CURIOUS DORSET

DORSET

DERRICK WARREN

BOURNEMOUTH
2004
LIBRARIES

BOU

D1079091

First published in the United Kingdom in 2004 by
Sutton Publishing Limited · Phoenix Mill
Thrupp · Stroud · Gloucestershire · GL5 2BU

Copyright © Derrick Warren, 2004

All rights reserved. No part of this publication may be reproduced, stored in a retrieval system, or transmitted, in any form, or by any means, electronic, mechanical, photocopying, recording or otherwise, without the prior permission of the publisher and copyright holder.

Derrick Warren has asserted the moral right to be identified as the author of this work.

British Library Cataloguing in Publication Data
A catalogue record for this book is available from the British Library.

ISBN 0-7509-3733-5

Typeset in 11/13.5pt Janson.
Typesetting and origination by
Sutton Publishing Limited.
Printed and bound in England by
J.H. Haynes & Co. Ltd, Sparkford.

CONTENTS

Wreckage and corpses from a stricken vessel being washed ashore below Church Cliffs, Lyme Regis. This print by J.M.W. Turner was accidentally inserted into the wrong volume of his *Picturesque Views of England and Wales* (1836), and is annotated 'Lyme Regis, Norfolk'!

AUTHOR'S NOTE

This book does not set out to be a comprehensive guide to Dorset or a history of the county – that has already been done by far more knowledgeable writers. This is simply a personal and idiosyncratic collection of entirely unrelated facts and stories about places and people remembered from knowing and loving the county since childhood and having worked in it for many years as a (very inquisitive) Ordnance Surveyor.

With three exceptions (which are acknowledged) and one that I came across this year, I knew of all the subjects covered but I did not know all about them, so it has been an interesting and enjoyable exercise in putting some flesh on those long-remembered bones and revisiting every site, many not seen for a long time. Where I have digressed it is because the 'aside' amused me, caught my imagination or gives added colour or a different slant to a subject. Some places have a connection with a person, or a person with a place, however slight, and these have been dealt with briefly within the subject-matter. Churches I have largely passed over (they have been done splendidly by Pevsner and others) in favour of what they and their churchyards contain – for there history lies! Where a town or village is not mentioned, or only briefly, it does not mean that there is nothing of interest, just that I did not know of it; neither, for the same reason, have I tried to balance the entries across the county.

For locals I hope that I have jogged a few memories, and for visitors that I have shown the unusual or little-known aspects of this beautiful part of England. The entries have been numbered alphabetically by location, with their prefix numbers corresponding to those on the index map. Most can be visited or viewed from a public road or footpath, and the map references should enable them to be found easily (Ordnance Survey Landranger Series, sheets 183, 193, 194 and 195). However, even though a map reference is given it does not necessarily mean that there is public access – in those instances I have tried to make that clear in the text.

Except where individually acknowledged, all the photographs and illustrations are from my own collection.

Derrick Warren
Taunton, 2004

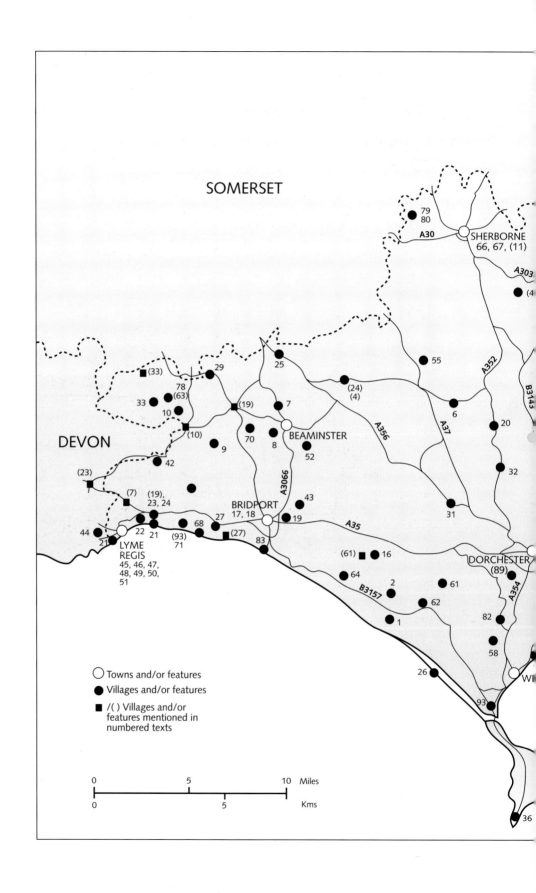

SOMERSET

DEVON

BRIDPORT
17, 18

BEAMINSTER

SHERBORNE
66, 67, (11)

LYME
REGIS
45, 46, 47,
48, 49, 50,
51

DORCHESTER
(89)

A30

A303

A352

B3143

A37

A356

A3066

A35

B3157

A354

79
80

(4

55

(24)
(4)

29

25

(33)

78
(63)

33

10

(19)

7

6

20

(10)

70

8

9

52

32

42

43

(23)

31

(7)

(19),
23, 24

19

44

22   21

68

27

(27)

83

(93)
71

21

(61)   16

64

2

61

62

82

1

58

26

WI

93

36

○ Towns and/or features
● Villages and/or features
■ /( ) Villages and/or
   features mentioned in
   numbered texts

0   5   10   Miles
├────────┼────────┤
0   5   Kms

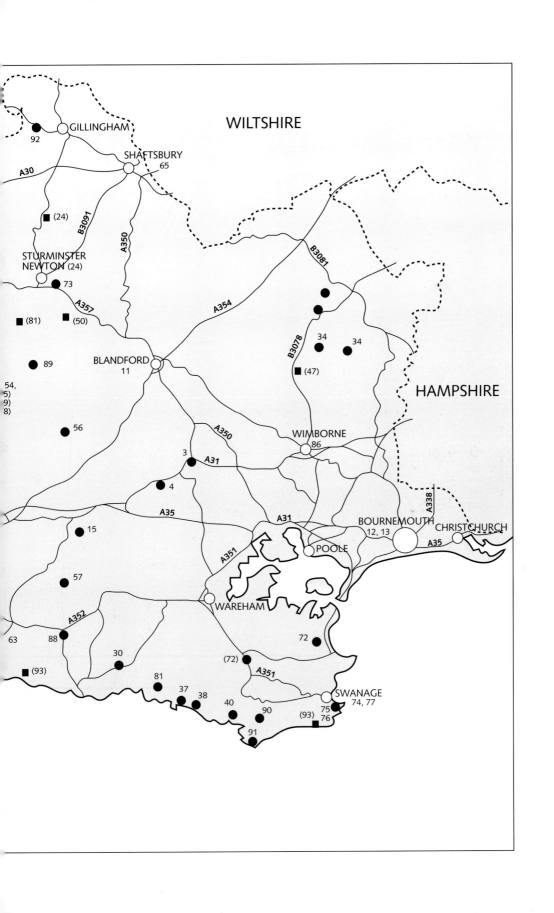

CURIOSITIES

ABBOTSBURY

The Chapel on the Hill

1

Map Ref
SY 572846

The Pilgrim Chapel of St Catherine, *c.* 1400, stands prominently on a bare hilltop south of Abbotsbury overlooking the wide sweep of Lyme Bay. Once a part of the great Benedictine Abbey at Abbotsbury, it survived the Dissolution of the Monasteries, *c.* 1539, because it was useful, both as a watch-tower and as a landmark for shipping in the Bay. The chapel is only 41ft long and 15ft wide, and has a curved, tunnel-vault ceiling supporting the stone-clad roof. There is a little oratory in the short tower and the doors are the only features made of wood in the whole building. The windows were glazed in the nineteenth century. With its earthen floor, no lighting and the wind whistling through its doors, its remoteness is breathtaking.

St Catherine is the patron saint of spinsters (women of the family who spun the wool for weaving) and on her Feast Day, 25 November, spinsters would come here to pray for a husband.

> A Husband, St Catherine
> A handsome one, St Catherine
> A rich one, St Catherine
> A nice one, St Catherine
> And soon, St Catherine

A few services are held here throughout the year, including one at 3 p.m. on 25 November.

St Catherine's Chapel, looking inland to Wear's Hill and Abbotsbury Castle.

2

Map Ref
SY 557879

ABBOTSBURY

A Chapel in the Woods

Only 2 miles to the north of St Catherine's Chapel, hidden deep in the Ashley Woods, are the ruins of St Luke's Chapel, slightly smaller than St Catherine and with only one wall standing, but 200 years older.

The Cistercian Abbey at Netley on Southampton Water, had a 'grange', or farm, on this site in 1245, worked by a few monks and lay brothers. The chapel for them was built above a small stream, with a large pond close by (a fish pond?), now silted up to just a bog. With the abbey empty after the Dissolution, the community was abandoned, the woods grew around it and it faded into obscurity, until, in 1925, the Ashley property was bought by Sir David and Lady Olga Milne-Watson, who built a new home nearby, Ashley Chase.

The Milne-Watsons fell in love with the little ruined chapel and had one of their workmen conserve what remained (he, in ignorance, made the window in the west gable-end into a doorway) and had a stone altar and a wooden cross erected at the east end (there is now a stone cross). When they died they were both buried there.

The chapel is no longer consecrated, and because of its inaccessibility to all but the sure-footed the yearly Easter Service, held there until recently, no longer takes place, but there is still the occasional wedding blessing or baptism. On the east bank of the nearby track there is a stile leading into the woods, which in spring are carpeted with primroses and bluebells.

3

Map Ref
SY 970883

ALMER

The Ring Road

Near the hamlet of Almer the main road from Dorchester to Wimborne Minster follows, in a wide sweeping curve, the brick wall bounding the northern side of Charborough Park, and is well known to motorists for the two massive gateways, one surmounted by a stag and the other a lion. The road once used to go right through the middle of Charborough Park, but in 1841 the owner, J.S.W.S. Erle Drax, wanting privacy, had the road closed to the public. This resulted in legal proceedings being instituted by a Dorchester man, who lost the case. The old road was closed and a new one built around the perimeter of the park. In triumph, Drax had an inscription placed on the entrance lodge proclaiming his victory, but he had it placed facing inwards so that the public using the road could not see it! The park is still extremely private.

St Luke's Chapel with Sir David's and Lady Olga's graves.

ANDERSON

'Red Post'

4

Map Ref
SY 970883

Felons sentenced to transportation had to walk from the court where they were sentenced to the nearest port of embarkation to Australia, and were expected to cover about 18 miles in a day. On routes used regularly arrangements were made with farmers for the prisoners to spend the night in a barn; however, the escorting warders/soldiers were often illiterate so, to indicate to them where to turn off the main road to go to such a barn, the finger post was painted red.

Here, on the road from Dorchester to Wimborne, there was a farm used by the authorities about a quarter of a mile down a lane leading to Bloxworth, with the finger post at the Anderson junction painted red. The farm became known as Botany Bay Farm, and although the original farm has been demolished and new buildings and house erected, the name has been kept. After transportation ceased the finger post continued, by tradition, to be painted red, and still is to this day, with the junction becoming simply Red Post. The name Botany Bay has been appropriated by a public house and a filling station about half a mile along the road to Wimborne.

The old-style fingerpost with the NG map reference below 'Red Post' on the circle.

There is a similar red-painted direction post on the road from Beaminster to Evershot at ST 553039, where a lane turns off to Hemlock Farm, and although local knowledge has it that here too prisoners being sent from gaol to gaol would turn off for the night, nothing is said about hemlock being dispensed there for those desperate enough! Just over the county border into Somerset, near Chard, there is another 'Red Post' at a crossroads, and here, about half a mile away, there was an isolated barn, demolished in about 1938, which was always known as 'Red Barn' because it was limewashed red.

BADBURY RINGS

The Beech Avenue

For 2¼ miles the road from Blandford to Wimborne, near Badbury Rings, is bordered by a splendid avenue of now venerable beech trees, 365 on each side, one for every day of the year, although time and the elements have taken their toll but not, so far, the County Council. It was reputedly planted by a forester on the Kingston Lacy Estate in 1838, and is the longest avenue in Europe. A third row of young beech trees has now been planted parallel to and 20 yards to the north-east of the avenue – does this presage a future road widening?

5

Map Ref
ST 960027

BATCOMBE HILL

The Cross and Hand Stone

Standing isolated beside the road the round, 3ft 6in high stone was once surmounted by a cross and, with a little imagination, the outline of a hand can still be made out. Its true history has been lost in the mists of time but it is thought to be Roman in origin and brought here (when the then unfenced track crossed bare downland) either as a waymark or as a boundary stone, although no boundary exists near it today. It has been suggested that the stone marks the spot where a murderer lies buried having first sold his soul to the Devil, but for centuries it has been an object of curiosity.

6

Map Ref
ST 037630

The Cross and Hand Stone. The hand is just discernible.

7

Map Ref
ST 467031

BEAMINSTER

Under the Hill

The turnpike road from Bridport to Crewkerne, established by the second Bridport Turnpike Trust in 1764, was built to further trade between Bridport and its hinterland, particularly flax and twine for its rope and net industry. A mile north of Beaminster the road had to climb steeply over Horn Hill and so, to ease the route, Giles Russell, of Beaminster, conceived the idea of a tunnel to go through the hill. His enthusiasm for the scheme encouraged support, and Mr M. Lane, a pupil of Brunel, was engaged as engineer for the project. It was said that Mr Lane had been a pupil of Isambard Kingdom Brunel (b. 1806) but it is more likely that he was under Isambard's father, Sir Marc (b. 1764), who was a known tunnel engineer (his famous Thames Tunnel was completed in 1842). At that date Isambard was yet to make his name with his tunnels for the Great Western Railway. Work commenced on the Horn Hill Tunnel in August 1832 and was completed only ten months later in June 1833. Approached by deep cuttings, the tunnel is 115yds long, 20ft high and 18ft wide, with a brick lining and portals. It was provided with two oil lamps, one at each end, with the nearby toll-house keeper acting as lamplighter. The project was marred by an accident which killed a workman, William Aplin, 'killed by a quantity of earth falling on him in widening the road under the hill this side (south) of the tunnel'. The stone plaques set over the portals read: 'The public are principally indebted for the erection of this Tunnel to the exertions of

The south portal of Horn Hill Tunnel, c. 1909.

The north portal of Thistle Hill Tunnel, *c.* 1906, from *Where Dorset Meets Devon*.

Giles Russell of Beaminster Gent. Begun August eighteenth 1831. Finished June 1832. M. Lane Civil Engineer.'

There is a similar tunnel under Thistle Hill, on the Charmouth to Axminster road built by the same Trust. It is longer, 220yds, but identical in every other respect, and although there are no plaques over the portals it must be assumed that Mr Lane was the engineer. This tunnel has now been bypassed by a new road and is blocked to vehicles, but it can be seen and walked through – with difficulty! Road tunnels are rare in this country, and to have two in one area is remarkable.

8

Map Ref
ST 468008

BEAMINSTER

Daniel's Plot

James Daniel, a Beaminster lawyer, joined the Duke of Monmouth's cause at Lyme Regis and, after the Duke's defeat on Sedgemoor, fled home to Beaminster with a price on his head and the King's soldiers hard on his heels. He had to hide in a barn about a mile short of Beaminster, and burrowed down under the hay; the soldiers were convinced that he was nearby so they trampled all over the hay, prodding it with their bayonets and pikes. Miraculously, they all missed James and he escaped. After four years, when the hounding of Monmouth's supporters had died down, James, in thanksgiving to God for his deliverance, bought the barn and a piece of adjoining ground as a burial plot for him and his descendants. It was some time before it was used, however, for James lived to the ripe old age of 100, dying in 1711. The plot stands alone amid the fields, and is some 40ft by 20ft, surrounded by a sturdy field hedge built, it is said, with stone from the barn. By 1860 there had been many burials and the ground was then consecrated, with stone gate pillars and heavy double iron gates put up; these are now kept locked but the key can be obtained from nearby Knowle Farm.

The gates to Daniel's plot.

BETTISCOMBE

The Screaming Skull

9

Map Ref
ST 401003

At Bettiscombe Manor there is the skull of a Negro. If it is moved out of the house, screams are said to be heard. Although embellished over the years, the story, as told to me by my father and as it was told to him in 1911 by the then owner, a Mr Pinney, is as follows. An ancestor of Mr Pinney was a supporter of Monmouth and in 1685, after Monmouth's defeat at Sedgemoor, he fled to the West Indies where he settled, made a small fortune, married and had children and grandchildren. Eventually one of his grandsons returned to their old home, bringing with him a servant, a Negro slave. This servant was assured that he would be freed and allowed to return to his native land to die and be buried there; whether by deliberate intent or by unforeseen circumstances that promise was not, or could not, be kept. The old Negro died, but before he did so he put a curse on the house and its occupants, saying that should he be taken from the house his screams would be heard and the house would rock! Nevertheless, he was buried in the local churchyard screams were heard and the house did shake; eventually he was exhumed and his skull taken into the house, whereupon the screams ceased and the house was at peace.

The belief arose that should the skull be ever removed from the house again the owner would be dead within the year; superstition or not, the skull has never been removed. Over the years many other

Bettiscombe Manor, *c.* 1906, from *Where Dorset Meets Devon.*

stories have grown up around it: that it was thrown into a pond and that when it surfaced 'the house rocked to its foundations'; it was buried deep in a midden but within days it had risen to the top and the screams commenced; that the Negro was versed in voodoo or that the 'happenings' are all down to auto-suggestion. However, after 250 years the skull is still there in its cardboard box! It must be emphasised that Bettiscombe is strictly private and that the skull is *never* on view to the public.

Friar Waddon Manor, near Portisham, also had a skull that moaned, but this one is now safely tucked away in the cellar of Dorset County Museum.

BIRDSMOORGATE

The Devil's Three Jumps

10

Map Ref
ST 3801

High on the ridge between Birdsmoorgate (ST 391009) and Sadborow (ST 372020) are three clumps of beech trees known as The Devil's Three Jumps. These were probably planted by the Bragge family to commemorate the rebuilding of their home, Sadborow, in 1778 after it had burnt down. These clumps were once visible for miles around but are now, sadly, partly obscured by plantations of firs. The story goes that the Devil had to take three giant strides to jump into Devon and that the trees were planted on the imprints made by his feet! Was he being chased out of Dorset by the Cow and her Calf, as Pilsdon Pen and Lewesdon Hill were once called by sailors who used them as landmarks when sailing in the Channel. It is also interesting that while place-names just over the border in Devon are Godly – Heaven's Gate, Holy City, Paradise – in Dorset the Devil prevails – with the Agglestone, the Devil's Bellows and Devil's Toenails, the local name given to Gryphea, a fossil found on Charmouth beaches.

The unusually named Birdsmoorgate is an interesting example of an old name being corrupted (possibly by an early Ordnance Surveyor from London!). It was originally Furze Moor Gate, literally meaning a gate across a lane that became an unfenced track crossing rough open heathland – a furze moor.

BLANDFORD FORUM

Monument to the Great Fire

Fires were common in towns, with their thatched houses and crowded-in streets, but the fire that started at 2 p.m. in a tallow-chandler's house in Blandford on 4 June 1731 was the 'Great Fire'. Three-quarters of the town was consumed, 480 families lost their homes and 74 inhabitants perished; when even the little wooden fire-engines were burnt the weary townsfolk had to see their church go likewise.

But the fire has left Blandford as the most wonderfully complete Georgian town in England, thanks to two brothers, John and William

Blandford's memorial to its great fire.

Bastard, who were appointed overseers to its rebuilding, who designed some of it themselves but influenced all the remainder. Not with such grand buildings as at Bath, but with small, elegant town houses, rows of cottages, inns and public buildings, including a new, light and airy church of St Peter and St Paul.

By the west front of the church is a pillared monument to the fire:

In remembrance of God's dreadful Visitation by Fire which broke out on 4th June 1731 and in a few hours reduced, not only the Church and almost the whole Town to Ashes. Herein 74 inhabitants perished but also two adjacent villages. To the Grateful Acknowledgement of the DIVINE MERCY that has since raised the town like the PHOENIX from the Ashes to its present, beautiful and flourishing State. Also to Prevent, by a timely supply of water (with God's Blessing) the future consequences of FIRE hereafter. This MONUMENT of this dire DISASTER and provision against the like, is humbly erected by John Bastard, a considerable sufferer in the general calamity. 1760

Underneath another tablet says: 'The old pump was substituted by the present fountain by the Corporation of Blandford Forum. 1899.'

John Bastard must also have believed that 'God helps those who help themselves' for a further inscription says that in 1768 he gave '£100 to keep the pump in repair and supplying an oil lamp with oil and a man to light the same every night from Michaelmas to Lady Day for Ever'. However, 'for Ever' must have been abandoned when the old pump was replaced by the drinking fountain.

The Fire Bell in Sherborne Abbey Church, rung only for major outbreaks of fire in the town, is inscribed, probably by someone who also held Bastard's belief:

Lord, quench this furious flame
Arise, run, help put out the same.

BOURNEMOUTH

The Making of a Resort

12

Map Ref
SZ 09/19

Since the thirteenth century Poole had been a thriving port but its neighbour, Bournemouth, only a few miles east along the coast, was a tiny fishing hamlet. During the early part of the nineteenth century its miles of sands, its bracing air and the healthy smell of the pinewoods growing along the cliffs changed all that and the area became a mecca for the disabled and invalids, particularly popular with those suffering from consumption and similar complaints. Villas, hotels, nursing homes and sanatoriums sprang up, leading one eminent medical man to comment that 'one sees more crutches and invalid chairs here than anywhere else in England'! Countless celebrated people came there for their health, some staying only a few months, others years. Among the latter was Robert Louis Stevenson (1850–87) who lived at Skerrymore, 61 Alum Chine Road, from 1884 to 1887 (with his consumption and 'smoker's cough') and where he completed *Kidnapped* and wrote *The Strange Case of Dr. Jekyll and Mr. Hyde*. Skerrymore (named after one of his uncle's Scottish lighthouses) was damaged by a German bomb in 1940 and was demolished in the 1950s to become the Robert Louis Stevenson Memorial Garden.

Bournemouth, 1853.

13

Map Ref
SY 09/19

BOURNEMOUTH

A Cabinet of Curiosities

The drawing together into 'encyclopædias' of the whole of the world's knowledge goes back as far as Aristotle, and over the centuries collections of artefacts supplemented and illustrated this knowledge; these collections became known as 'cabinets of curiosities' – the precursors to today's museums. From the eighteenth century onwards, with travel becoming progressively easier and cheaper and with many more books and information available, collecting became the vogue among the more educated classes in society, although this collecting was rarely along specific or scientific lines. These collections did indeed become 'cabinets of curiosities' with a wide range of disparate items proclaiming their owner's travels, tastes or degree of wealth. With the rise of the middle-classes during the nineteenth century the more affluent showed off their Venetian glass, *objets d'art* or foreign 'curios' in glass-fronted cabinets, while in humbler homes the Goss china, seashells or other knick-knacks were displayed on the mantelshelf.

Bournemouth can boast that it not only has one of the largest such collections in the country but a most unusual 'cabinet' in which they are displayed – East Cliff Hall – now the Russell-Cotes Museum and Art Gallery. East Cliff Hall was built by Sir Merton and Lady Russell-Cotes, both to live in and to display their collections. Completed in 1901, just before Queen Victoria died, it was built with all the confidence and aspirations of the burgeoning *nouveau riche*, and in Sir Merton's own words 'it combines the renaissance and Italian with old Scottish baronial styles'. During the twentieth century this style of architecture fell out of fashion in this country and East Cliff Hall is a rare survivor, although in America many such houses still exist.

East Cliff Hall's interior is as singular as its exterior, for each room has its own distinctive colour scheme and many are decorated to illustrate a country or place that Sir Merton and Lady Russell-Cotes had visited; an alcove is decorated in Moorish style as a reminder of their visit to Spain, while another reflects Japan with a superb collection of nineteenth-century Japanese silver. One room is given over to memorabilia of Sir Henry Irving, a lifelong friend of the Russell-Cotes, with his make-up box of grease-paints, the skull he used when playing *Hamlet*, a lock of his hair and his death mask. Other rooms, 'cabinets' in themselves, have also glass display cases showing off such diverse objects as a plaster cast of Lady Hamilton's hand, the milk teeth of Lady Russell-Cotes' grandchildren mounted on a pendant and a tiny envelope containing ash from the crater of a live volcano in Hawaii, collected by Sir Merton himself. There are models of Japanese wrestlers, Palestinian head-dress and bridal shoes, an arrangement of feathers as art from Rio de Janeiro, stuffed birds from all over the world, including the now extinct kea from New Zealand and a large case of mounted butterflies. The bizarre list goes on and on!

To cap all this, the walls of every room, the hallways and staircase are literally clothed with pictures and there is a statuette or bronze bust on every available surface, including some marble and bronze statues by Pietro Calvi, for the Russell-Cotes were keen collectors of art – even to the extent of building three additional galleries after they had made over the house and all its collections to Bournemouth Corporation in 1908.

The paintings are mostly by Victorian artists, many of whom are only now coming back into favour. Some are huge; *Approaching Thunderstorm in Picardy* by Henry W. Bank Davies, RA, (*c.* 1869) takes up almost a whole wall, while a delightfully life-like study entitled *Gypsy Horse Drovers*, by Lucy Kemp-Welsh, is nearly as big. There is Albert Moore's *Midsummer*; William Etty's *Dawn of Love*; Landseer's *A Highland Flood*; Henry Justice Ford's faithful copy of Anna Lee Merritt's *Love Locked Out*, to mention only a few of the hundreds on view. It is said that Sir Merton thought Byam Shaw's *Jezebel* showed rather too much flesh and had drapes painted on to it, although he, like other Victorian gentlemen, did buy other 'classical' studies of the lightly draped female!

All in all this is a surprising treasure house, to compare with the Sir John Soane Museum and the Horniman, both in London. Open Tuesdays to Sundays 10 a.m. to 5 p.m., it is not to be passed by, especially as admission is free. One can only echo a comment in the *Bournemouth Observer* in 1895, while Sir Merton was Mayor: 'a man on whose importance everybody dotes / Give three cheers for F.R.C.S. Merton Russell-Cotes!'

East Cliff Hall, now the Russell-Cotes Museum and Art Gallery.

14

Map Ref
SY 705819

BOWLEAZE

The Riveria Hotel

To the east of the little River Jordan, where it flows into Weymouth Bay, is a marvellous example of 1930s architecture – the Riveria Hotel. The single-storeyed arcaded front, with its central tower, was built entirely of reinforced concrete and its eighth of a mile-long, crescent-shaped frontage, besides looking decidedly Moorish, acted as a sun trap. It was one of the most modern hotels on the south coast and had the largest dance hall in the country, as well as other indoor and outdoor recreational facilities. It was designed by a local architect, L. Stewart Smith, of Weymouth, who went on to build many other hotels.

The building is startlingly white against the backdrop of green Dorset coastal downland and even though a second arcaded storey has been added (in the same style), because it is still low it does not intrude upon the landscape (as do so many modern buildings) but has become part of it.

The River Jordan at Bowleaze, with Portland in the background, as it was in about 1890. *From an original watercolour by Margaret Derrick.*

The Riviera Hotel, *c.* 1938, before the second storey was added.

The Riviera Hotel as it is today.

15

Map Ref
SY 812933

BRIANTSPUDDLE

A War Memorial

On the outskirts of the small village of Briantspuddle, in the centre of an open gravel space with a tree-lined driveway concealing the Arts and Crafts-style thatched 'cottages' of Bladen Valley, is the tall (about 30ft), slender memorial to the war dead of the parish. On one side of the memorial is the figure of Christ holding a downward-pointing sword, facing out over the water-meadows of the River Trent, and on the other, facing up the drive, is a small statue of a seated Madonna and Child, under a pillared canopy.

What makes these sculptures so beautiful and memorable is their simplicity and strength of form, for the whole was the work of that incomparable 1920s sculptor and calligrapher, Eric Gill. Around the plinth are carved the strangely philosophical words: 'It is sooth that sin is cause of all this pain. But all shall be well And all manner of thing shall be well.'

Briantspuddle can be proud, not only of a glorious tribute to its dead, but to whoever commissioned it as well.

Eric Gill's war
memorial at
Briantspuddle.

BRIDE VALLEY

'An Agricultural Workers Dwelling'

Driving up the beautiful and remote valley of the little River Bride towards Bridehead House, rebuilt in 1847 in 'Strawberry Hill Gothic', one passes Kingston Russell, a restored Queen Anne house where Admiral Hardy was born. Just past it, on rounding a corner, one is confronted by a small but imposing Georgian–Irish country house – Bellamont – set in an unspoilt dip in the downs. One can be forgiven for not realising that it was only built in 1996 as the 'farmhouse' for an open farm of 140 acres, or, as the planning consent stated, 'for an agricultural workers dwelling'! However, in the 1997 Government Planning Policy Guidelines which set out to protect green-field sites from development, paragraph 3.21 stated 'an isolated house in the countryside may also exceptionally be justified if it is clearly of the highest quality, is truly outstanding in terms of its architecture and landscape design and would sympathetically enhance its immediate and wider surroundings . . .'. Eventually Bellamont will merge into the surrounding landscape and in a hundred years' time it will, perhaps, be open to the public as an 'historic' house – or even taken over by the National Trust as an example of how a farm worker lived at the end of the twentieth century!

The 'agricultural workers' dwelling, 1997.

17

BRIDPORT

. . . of Rope-makers and Quakers

Bridport's broad streets are no accident of building, no early concept in town planning, but grew from their use over the centuries as open-air rope walks, each sited conveniently outside the fronts of the rope-makers' houses. As far back as King John (1199–1216), who ordered hemp cables for his ships from Bridport, rope, twine and net-making was the mainstay of the local economy. Six hundred years later the famous landscape artist, J.M.W. Turner, was to muse:

> . . . that low-sunk town
> Whose trade has flourished from early time
> Remarkable the thread called Bridport twine.

And remarkable was one use to which it was put, besides that on ships; for it became notorious as gallows rope. In fact, it was said of budding miscreants 'You'll live to be stabbed with a Bridport Dagger', that being the macabre name given to the gallows in the sixteenth century. Leland, in his *Itinerary* (a record of his journeys through England between 1533 and 1545) reported – whether because he was unaware of the true meaning of the expression or, more likely, in appreciative jest, '. . . in Bridport be made good daggers'!

Away from the bustling broad streets of present-day Bridport, an oasis of peace can be found down a passageway on the east side of South Street, where the Meeting House, the snug old almshouses and the little burial ground of the Bridport Quakers are located. The Quakers have met here since 1690 when they were allowed the use of a barn for their meetings. The barn belonged to Daniel Taylor who seven years later gave it to them, together with a small plot of land for burials, for, being Dissenters, they were not allowed to use the church graveyard. On his death Taylor's house and tenements became almshouses, although not exclusively for the use of Quakers, and the whole site remains today much as it was 300 years ago. The Meeting House, as are all Friends' Meeting Houses (Quakers are now generally known as 'Friends'), is simple, with white walls, plain wooden benches or chairs, a raised dais for the elders but no decoration or focal point, for there is no minister or order of service; Friends meet in silence, with each responding in their own way. The Meeting House is always open for quiet meditation and the little burial ground as a haven of peace.

A courtyard in Bridport, with the Friends' Meeting House on the right, almshouses on the left and the little burial ground down the alleyway.

18

Map Ref
SY 465921

BRIDPORT

The Thatched Brewery

Small, old-established town breweries are, nowadays, few and far between, but Palmer's Brewery in Bridport is exceptional, for it boasts that it has the only thatched brewery building in the country. Of course, since the brewery started in 1794 it has grown, brewing technology has advanced and the beer is no longer brewed in those original buildings, although the bottling plant is still 'under the thatch'. The site was originally a corn mill on the confluence of the little Asker and Brit rivers, and had several proprietors before being taken over by two brothers – John Cleeves Palmer and Robert Henry Palmer – in 1896, with the family name still on the Board of Directors. The pumps in the brewery were first worked by a waterwheel; the last replacement, an 18ft diameter iron undershot wheel made by T. Helyer in 1879, can be seen from the bridge on the side road to Eype. There are tours of the brewery during the summer months, the times of which can be obtained from the adjoining shop.

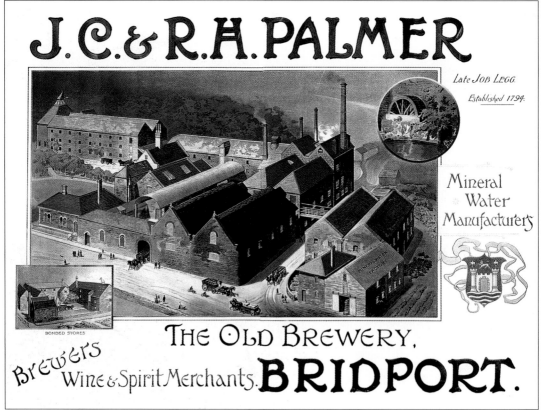

Trade advertisement of Palmer's Brewery, *c.* 1920. The old thatched brewery is clearly visible centre foreground. *(Courtesy of Palmer's Brewery)*

BRIDPORT

The King Charles Stone

About half a mile out of Bridport on the Dorchester road, where Lee Lane joins it, there is a rough stone monument, erected in 1901, which marks the spot where the course of English history could so easily have been changed.

On Tuesday 23 September 1651 Charles Stuart, the future King Charles II, had failed to secure a boat at Charmouth to take him to France after his defeat at Worcester, and, having taken breakfast at the George Inn at Bridport, was on his way, via Dorchester, back to Trent Manor, near Sherborne, where Col Wyndham would harbour him. On an impulse the party turned down Lee Lane to go instead via Broadwindsor, little knowing that the Parliamentary troops pursuing them were only minutes behind. Had they not turned off then Charles would almost certainly have been captured and executed. The Revd Thomas Fuller, Vicar of Broadwindsor, wrote a contemporary account of the incident 'in which he [Charles] had not rode past half a mile, ere by a finger of Divine Provenance, was directed down a narrow lane by which means (though they knew not wither they went) they were safely conducted to Broadwindsor . . .'.

There is an inscription on the stone, now much eroded, which reads: 'King Charles II Escaped Capture through this lane Sept. XVIII, MDCLI' with the couplet 'From midst your fiercest foes on every side, for your escape God did a Lane provide.'

With the exception of two small stone plaques on the walls of the Queen's Arms Hotel at Charmouth and on a former inn at Broadwindsor, this is the only reminder of Charles' travels through Dorset.

The King Charles Stone, *c.* 1923. Today the inscription is indecipherable.

20

Map Ref
ST 666016

CERNE ABBAS

The Giant

This is undoubtedly the best-known chalk hill-figure in England, but authorities differ as to its age and who it represents. It was long thought to have been a pagan fertility figure, an Iron-age god-warrior or the Greek god Hercules, but, surprisingly, there is no mention of him until 1754 when he was recorded by the Revd Richard Proctor – one would have thought that such an upstanding figure of a man would have warranted a mention long before that! Current thinking is that the figure may be a caricature of Oliver Cromwell or a bucolic jibe against the Puritans, for it was much disliked by the local clergy of that time who tried to get it grassed over.

Myths invariably grow up around any unusual object and the Giant is no exception. It was believed that should a couple be childless then a sure way to conceive would be to make love on the tip of the Giant's phallus. (There is a certain truth in this, for conception is more likely if the woman is lying head down at 45°, however uncomfortable that might be!) Should that fail then there was another, more discreet, way.

The Giant.

In the grounds of the old Cerne Abbas Priory there is a spring – St Augustine's Well. It is said that St Augustine, on a pilgrimage in this part of the country, came across some shepherds, and as it was a hot day asked them which they would prefer to drink – ale or water. Knowing what was politic to say they asked for water, whereupon St Augustine struck the ground with his staff and water gushed out from the spot. The water from this spring (for a long time the village water supply) was thought to have curative properties, one of which was to increase a woman's fertility.

St Augustine's Well.

21

Map Ref
SY 36490 &
SY 335915

CHARMOUTH

Factories on the Beach

Today the cliffs and beaches around Charmouth and Lyme Regis resound to the chink of hammers as visitors search for fossils; 150 years ago they would have resounded to the chink of pick-axes, the thump of explosives and the noise of steam engines grinding stone, and would have been covered by thick palls of smoke and dust from the burning lime kilns. Then the cliffs and shore were a cheap and easily accessible source of lias limestone and clay for making hydraulic cement and bricks. The old factory on the beach at Charmouth is now known for its heritage centre and café; it was built, however, in about 1854 by the Plymouth firm of John Morcombe & Son, specifically to manufacture hydraulic cement. Lias stones washed from the cliffs were collected by horse and cart, broken into small pieces, mixed with culm and clay and then burnt in kilns, one of which can still be seen behind the factory. Once the mixture had been burnt (calcined) it was crushed by two large, vertical runner-stones, revolving in a circular stone trough, powered by a small steam engine. (These stones, each weighing over a ton, are now mounted on either side of a seat on the cliff above the factory.) The culm to burn the stone would have been landed from barques beached at high tide and the cement taken away by the same means. The coast and weather did not favour this method of transportation and the venture failed after a

Cement Factory, Charmouth, c. 1880. Note the Napoleonic defence cannons. *(Courtesy of The Pavey Group, Charmouth)*

short time, with the factory becoming for many years a store for the local fishermen. In about 1900 the chimney was demolished and the north end of the building had to be lowered because of cracks in the masonry.

It was a different story at Lyme Regis. Although in 1826 two brothers, W. & G.H. Stevens, were making and exporting hydraulic lime cement, it was the lias stone itself that was in demand, being widely exported for burning elsewhere. Such was the demand that the cliffs around the town were blasted down by explosives, causing concern about the safety of the church, to say nothing of the noise nuisance! A 'manufactory' for making cement and bricks was set up west of the Cobb in 1855 by Messrs Hutchinson & Frean, and the site continued to expand under different owners with, by 1913, between 60 and 100 men employed. The water needed in this production was provided by a huge pond on the cliff-top behind, and the works had two tall chimneys to carry away the smoke and fumes. By the 1930s the works had closed and in August 1935 the chimneys were brought down by the Royal Engineers, a great attraction for holiday-makers and locals alike! During the Second World War RAF Air-Sea Rescue Launches were based at Lyme and the old cement works buildings were converted into barracks and workshops. Little now can be seen of the site's former uses except the high earth dam of the now dry pond on the cliff-top and a length of iron trackway on the beach below the high-tide mark, some half a mile west of the old factory.

The Cobb, Lyme Regis, with cement factory and brickyard immediately below the cliff, *c.* 1910.

22

Map Ref
SY 352832

CHARMOUTH

The 'Devil's Bellows' and the Old Ways

Until about 300 years ago there were few roads as we know them in this part of the West Country; most were mere rough tracks only passable on foot or on horseback, with goods being carried by pack-horses. Celia Fiennes, riding on horseback in this area during her 'Great Journey' of 1698, said: 'The ways are difficult by reason of the very steep hills up and down . . . narrow and full of large round pebbles that make the strange horses slip and uneasy to go . . . the ways being very narrow they are forced to carry their corn on horse's backs with frames of wood like panniers on either side of the horses, so load them high and tie it with cords . . .'. Stukeley, writing twenty-five years later, noted 'the road following the coast was suitable only for horse-back riding'. Did he mean the old 'Roman' road which ran from Chideock via Stanton St Gabriel, up Stonebarrow Hill, down Stonebarrow Lane to Charmouth, then up over the cliffs (these have long slipped into the sea) to Timber Hill and down Colway Lane westwards – or was there a more direct route from Charmouth onwards? The problem with any road from Charmouth to Lyme was the instability of the 'stepped cliffs', making any 'undercliff' route extremely difficult. One such possible road turned off Higher Sea Lane in Charmouth, coming out above the almshouses at Lyme (on the present Charmouth Road) in what is now the short East Cliff Lane.

When the Bridport Turnpike Trust was established in 1758, it first improved the old 'Roman' road over the cliffs, but this had to be abandoned as a coach road because of its steepness and its exposure to the weather. In September 1825 a new coach road was built across the Undercliff, with a deep cutting at the Charmouth end to alleviate the steepness of the slope. This cutting soon became known as 'The Devil's Bellows' owing to the strength of the winds that blew through it! However, the Trust should have surveyed the terrain more thoroughly for three years later there was a landslip, causing a section of the road to drop 20ft. This was repaired and the road became so popular that it had to be widened twice, in 1839 and 1852. Disaster, however, struck on 26 May 1924 when a great landslip carried away most of the eastern part of the road and it was closed for good,

Profile map of the road from Lyme Regis to Bridport taken from a *Cyclists Touring Guide Book* of 1900, in which it was noted that 'cyclists in these parts need to be more than usually enthusiastic'! Horizontal distances are shown by the vertical lines in miles with heights given at 100ft intervals.

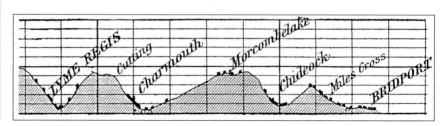

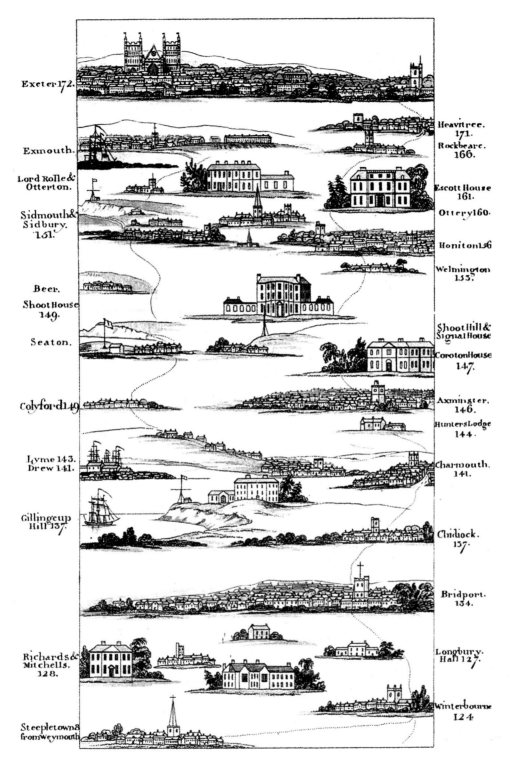

Section of a 'route map' from London to Exeter published by J. Baker in 1801. This sheet commences at Steepleton and not only shows the mileages from London, but also the prominent features (a signal station on Gillingcup Hill (Golden Cap) and the 'spy house' at Puncknowle), and for the socially curious traveller, the country seats of the local gentry.

Charmouth/Lyme Regis road, c. 1921, showing the 'Devil's Bellows' cutting.

The same road in 1926.

although for many years 'the old coach road', in spite of its many undulations, was used as a convenient footpath to Lyme.

The only way then out of Charmouth was up Fern Hill towards Penn. The County Council, now the roads authority, eased the sharp corner where Fern Hill met the road from Lyme to Penn; then constructed an entirely new road to Lyme, avoiding Timber Hill and sweeping down in a curving arc to Frost's Cottage at the top of Colway Lane. At that time this was a major undertaking, and the contractors used a narrow-gauge railway and a little steam engine to move the spoil and materials.

CHARMOUTH

The Duel

Duelling was introduced into this country from France during the sixteenth century but was always outside the law, and the participants, including their seconds, could be tried for manslaughter or murder. The last reported duel in this country was in 1852 – between two Frenchmen, of course!

In the churchyard of St Andrew's Church at Charmouth is the chest tomb of 'James Warden Esq. who fell in a duel 28th April 1792 in the 56 year of his age'. Warden had been out shooting with Mr Bond, a friend and neighbour, when a dispute arose as to who had shot a particular partridge. 'Strong language ensued', one thing led to another and the upshot was that Bond challenged Warden to a duel. Warden, who was no stranger to danger, having been in the Navy and fought in the American War of Independence, accepted. The duel took place near Hunters Lodge Inn, with Warden having a second – but Bond, because of the necessary secrecy, could not get one. Warden, the challenged, shot first, his ball going through Bond's hat; Bond then fired, his shot piercing Warden's

The duelist's tomb.

heart. The magistrates promptly charged Bond with murder and he fled the country. Warden's widow accepted that the duel was a matter of honour which had to be met, but was nevertheless heartbroken and had a verse composed by a Lyme man; this was inscribed on the tomb. Part of it reads:

> Dear victim of imperious honour's law
> These imperious laws enexorably stern
> Whose honour friendship views with
>   shuddering pause
> And love conubial shall for ever mourn . . .
> Adieu! in one alarming moment torn
> By ruffian rage, from her thy soul held dear . . .

24

Map Ref
SY 367937

CHARMOUTH

Damage this Bridge at your Peril

At the beginning of the nineteenth century Charmouth, being only 2 miles from Lyme Regis, had become an outpost of that town's gentility, with its main street, The Street, lined by superior, pretty houses. Jane Austen was a frequent visitor, noting that 'Charmouth with its high grounds and extensive sweeps of country, and, still more, its sweet retired bay, backed by dark cliffs, where fragments of low rock among the sands made it the happiest spot for watching the flow of tide, for sitting in unwearied contemplation'. She did not see, or if she did, she did not report on it, the distress that the recent collapse of the local economy had had on the hard-working labouring classes. A complete stranger to the area, passing through the nearby countryside in 1817, did see this and wrote: 'the wretched appearance of the cottages, the miserable situation . . . the comfortless order they are in; till within a short time, these poor people had good employment'. Around that time, even in such a respectable, genteel place as Charmouth, bad behaviour and lawlessness must have been present, otherwise why was there such such a stern warning on the parapet of Charmouth Bridge, at the bottom of The Street? 'Dorset. Any person wilfully injuring any part of this County Bridge will be guilt of felony and upon conviction liable to be transported for life. By the Court T. Fooks, 7&8 Geo. AC30 S13'.

Similar notices can be seen on Kings Mill Bridge at Sturminster Newton, Kings Stag Bridge, Benville Bridge and at Marnhull; two more are now in Devon, at Longbridge and Stockland, which were previously in Dorset.

On Charmouth
Bridge.

CHEDINGTON

Winyard's Gap

25
Map Ref
ST 491061

Where the old ridgeway road along Toller Down winds downwards to South Perrott, it does so through a gap in the hills – Winyard's Gap. But who was Winyard and why was it his gap? Was it some road-maker of long ago who had engineered the 'cutting' (for that is what it looks like) for a Turnpike Trust or older road? No one of that name has emerged; there is a vague reference to a Captain Winyard who brought his artillery over the hills during the Civil War, but that is all. According to one authority Winyard means 'whinn', a meadow and 'geard', an enclosure; another that 'whinn' means wine or vine, and 'geard' a garden, hence 'vineyard'; both are from the Old English and neither seems likely. Perhaps Vol. 4 of *Dorset Place Names* will provide an answer when it is eventually published. Or then again, perhaps the answer is simply that Winyard was once the name of the innkeeper at the hostelry there, giving both the gap and the inn their names?

CHESIL BEACH

26
Map Ref
SY 465901–
SY 682733

It is small wonder that the Dorset coast has been made a World Heritage site, not only for the range of rocks, fossils and scenery it can show from the Jurassic period, but because 10 miles of it are a comparatively recent geological feature unique in the world – a 'tombolo' or spit joined at both ends by land – the Chesil Bank, or as it is more commonly known, the Chesil Beach. (Old English 'ceosol'; 'cisel' – shingle.)

The origin of the Chesil Beach goes back to the Pleistocene period when it was built up under the sea and when the Fleet was a shallow river valley. Starting at West Bay, for the first 8 miles it is backed by low cliffs, except at Cogden where there is a mere. It is from Abbotsbury eastwards that the 'tombolo' begins for it is here that the Fleet, an almost tideless stretch of brackish water, divides it from the mainland. The Chesil Beach and the Fleet continue for another 10 miles until the beach joins Portland and the Fleet becomes tidal with an outlet, Small Mouth, into Weymouth Bay.

The statistics of the Chesil Bank are staggering: it consists of about 100 million tons of shingle; its crest at Abbotsbury is 22ft above mean high water and 43ft at Portland, and with cross-section widths at

Summer gale on the Chesil Bank, looking east from Burton beach.

Chesil Bank and the Fleet with St Catherine's Chapel in the middle distance left, looking west from Portland, c. 1935.

those points measuring 175ft and 220ft; its constituent material is graded in size along its length, with sand and fine shingle at West Bay to 2oz pebbles at Abbotsbury and 9oz 'cobbles' at Portland, and has a gradient on its seaward side of 1:2 to 1:9, depending on the weather conditions. Although there is a certain amount of beach movement eastwards little new material is now being added.

It is said that fishermen can tell their exact position on the beach by the size of the pebbles, and it is certainly true that the sound of the waves breaking on the shore changes from a whisper at West Bay, through a hissing at Abbotsbury, to rattling and rumbling at Portland.

The Fleet provides the suitable food and shelter for the famous swannery and great numbers of waterfowl, with many rare plants growing along its shoreline. The beach itself above the high tide lines gives ideal nesting conditions for two rare seabirds, the small and little terns, and this part of the beach is a protected area during their nesting season.

Even hardy walkers baulk at walking the length of the beach and there is no cliff path for many miles east of Abbotsbury. As for bathing off the beach – don't! For the backwash and undertow, even in relatively good weather, can be lethal.

CHIDEOCK

A Romanesque Church and a Jaw-bone Arch

27

Map Ref
SY 421933

Around 1280 John Gervase of Bridport was given the manor of Chideock (variously spelt Chidyoke or Chidwick) by his father, the family then taking the name 'de Chideock'. Shortly before the lands passed to cousins of the de Chideocks, the staunch Catholic and Royalist Arundells of Cornwall, Richard II (1373–99) granted John de Chideock 'licence to krenellate the manor there and build a castle there'. During the siege of Lyme Regis in the Civil War, about 1644, the castle was a thorn in the flesh of the Parliamentarians who eventually captured it, then lost it, only to take it yet again. After that the Parliamentarian commander at Lyme, Col Ceely, had the castle 'slighted' saying that 'he was stripping the feathers of the shuttlecock'. Nothing remains today of the castle since, as Dr Johnson said, 'walls supply stones more easily than quarries, and palaces and temples will be destroyed to build stables and cottages'.

For 170 years after the castle and its chapel were 'slighted' and the priest thrown out, the local Catholics had to resort to a barn to hold

The jaw-bone arch at Chideock.

their services. In 1802 Thomas Weld of Lulworth from another branch of the family, bought the estate for his son, Humphrey, who in 1815 built the present manor-house adjacent to the barn and made the barn more suitable for religious services. In 1872 Humphrey's son, Charles, had a new church erected on the site of the old barn, dedicated to St Mary the Virgin and St Ignatius. Although small it is built in an ornate Romanesque style reminiscent of churches in Tuscany, with an elaborately painted, domed sanctuary and a gilded Italian statue of Our Lady, top-lit by two small windows, which make it appear to be floating over the altar. Alien in style though it might be, it is, nevertheless, a delightful and beautiful surprise to find in a small rural Dorset village. Charles Weld, as Lord of the Manor, owned the foreshore rights at Seatown, which of course included all the flotsam and jetsam thrown up. In 1880 a whale became stranded on the beach, died, and after three days began to smell. Charles tried to have it burnt, but failed; he then had it cut up and the pieces disposed of (out at sea?). All, that is, except the whale's jaw-bones which were cleaned and taken to Chideock where they were erected as an arch over a wicket gate to a path leading to the manor-house. There they remain today, a little the worse for wear after 122 years but still standing, although the Weld family moved from the manor in 1996.

28

Map Ref
SY 670884

DORCHESTER

Maiden Castle

Today its towering ramparts merge into the landscape, but it is seldom mentioned what a visual impact Maiden Castle must have made during the period of its construction; the brilliant white of the freshly dug chalk proclaiming its size and strength for many miles around.

The enclosure on the summit is some 40 acres in extent but strangely, even during the last war when every square inch of suitable ground was put under the plough, it was never touched. Extensive excavation had taken place under Sir Mortimer Wheeler during 1935–7, when many graves of Belgic defenders killed by Vesparian's Roman Army, *c.* AD 44, were revealed, so little could have subsequently done any great harm on the surface. Ralph Wightman, the broadcaster and country writer, who had been a member of the local War Agricultural Executive Committee, maintained that it was superstition that prevented it from being disturbed yet again.

Sir Mortimer Wheeler's excavation of Maiden Castle during 1935–7. This photograph was taken with my first Box Brownie camera in 1936.

DRIMPTON

Picking Oakum

The long-disused Greenham Flax Mill at Drimpton can justly be called infamous, for it was here in the nineteenth century that children were employed in picking oakum – the pulling apart of short lengths of old rope into separate strands of hemp, to be re-used in the making of twine (the net-making industry of Bridport and area was the principal user of this twine). Until recently this activity was thought to have been given to convicts and the inmates of work-houses, to help maintain them and to occupy their time. It now transpires that Greenham Mill was one of only two recorded instances where children were used to do this soul-destroying task and get paid for doing so (in all likelihood a pittance). Clearly there must have been great poverty in the area for children to be so employed; times change, for now the mill houses a business catering for the needs of household pets! During the eighteenth and nineteenth centuries in the days of sail, any rigging and anchor ropes that were no longer usable became the 'perk' of the sailors, which they sold for oakum, hence the expression 'money for old rope'.

EAST LULWORTH

St Mary's (RC) Church

Lulworth Castle is what every child thinks a castle should look like – a fairy-tale castle, four-square with round angle-turrets at each corner. But it is a mock castle for it was built in 1608, long after castles were used for defensive purposes, and although gutted by fire in 1929 it has since been completely restored. In the grounds, however, is another building, erected in 1786, which in one sense is also mock, for it sets out to conceal its real use.

In 1641 the castle and lands passed into the hands of a Roman Catholic family, the Welds, who had, of course, to be discreet in practising their religion. Five years before the passing of the 'Catholic Reform Act' in 1791 (which allowed Roman Catholics to express their belief freely), it is said that King George III gave Thomas Weld permission to build a Catholic chapel at Lulworth provided it did not look like a church – so it doesn't!

It is not cruciform in shape, and from a distance its central dome makes it look like a mausoleum. Close up it resembles an eighteenth-

The truly disguised church at East Lulworth.

century country house, with Tuscan pillars beside the east and west doors. However, inside it is a serenely beautiful and superbly decorated church, with a pillared gallery on three sides and the sanctuary on the fourth with its carved marble altar surmounted by a carved ivory crucifix with lapis lazuli cross – all made in Italy. The painting on the inside of the dome depicts the Assumption of the Virgin Mary, while the floor is cool black and grey marble. In 1799 the chapel was given Royal approval when it was visited by King George III and Queen Charlotte on one of their visits to Dorset.

The castle and grounds are open to the public, and entry to the chapel is covered by the entrance fee.

FRAMPTON

A Porch

31

Map Ref
ST 630949

This unusual porch had originally been a small wooden summer-house, surmounted by a dovecote in the form of a spire, in the grounds of Frampton Court. When the court was demolished in 1932 it was dismantled and re-erected to serve as a porch tacked on to the end of a little thatched cottage in Frampton's main street. The holes for the nesting boxes have now been filled in but the Chinese reed ceiling in the summer-house, woven geometrically in a zig-zag pattern, has survived. Its charm now lies in the very incongruity with its surroundings.

A porch at Frampton.

32

Map Ref
SY 971666

GODMANSTONE

The Smith's Arms

The Smith's Arms claims to be the smallest public house in the country, being only 20ft long and 11ft wide, thatched and of only one storey.

Whether fact or fiction (or a bit of both) its history is interesting; 400 years ago King Charles II is said to have been passing nearby when his horse shed a shoe, so he had to stop at the nearest smithy. While waiting he asked for a drink; the smith gave him some ale but refused payment, saying that he could not charge as he had no licence, whereupon the King granted him a licence forthwith and so it has continued – no longer a smithy but still a public house.

Today it has an occasional licence, being only open from 12 noon to 5 p.m. during the spring and summer months.

The Smith's Arms,
c. 1930.

HOLDITCH

A Knight's Manor and its Chapel

On Dorset's extreme western border with Devon, Holditch Court was the only semi-fortified manor-house, in about 1400, in the county and was the home of Sir Thomas Brook (see **78**). Nothing remains of the house itself except one round angle tower, faced with knapped (squared) flint and, at 40ft, near its original height. There was a stairway inside but as a defensive measure there are no windows, only narrow

The ivy-covered tower at Holditch Court.

embrasures near the top. The tower now stands isolated (apart from modern farm buildings), romantically ivy-clad, overlooking a wide, peaceful sweep of the Axe Valley. There is no public access to the tower. The court was some 3 miles from the church at Thorncombe, and no doubt the little chapel at Holditch (ST 343026), less than half a mile away, would have been used by those living at the court, except perhaps on major church festivals. But why was the chapel not attached to the court as might have been expected, or indeed, as was normal? Perhaps the answer lies with the Cistercian Abbey at Ford (ST 359051), 2 miles to the north, for it could have been an out-chapel attached to the abbey, and dating from its founding in about 1137.

Thirteen monks had been dispatched in 1132 from the great Cistercian abbey at Waverley, in Surrey, to establish a new House of their Order at Brightley, in Devon, on land given to them by Richard de Redvers. After five fruitless years on that bleak and unproductive site they gave up to go back to Waverley, but, Redvers having died, they had to go and see Redvers' sister, Lady Alice, who lived at West Ford, to explain their failure. On the detour to see her they are said to have rested at Thorncombe, but this was more likely to have been at Holditch, which would have been on their direct route. Here they were met by Lady Alice who, saddened by her brother's poor gift, gave the monks, in exchange, her broad and fertile manor at West Ford, together with money to build their abbey at a place by the River Axe called Hartsbath. It is probable, therefore, that the little chapel at Holditch was built by the monks in remembrance of the gift and where it was offered. By 1900 the chapel had long been disused and was used as a barn; today it is just four walls, only a few feet high in places, but what does remain is conserved and listed.

The chapel at Holditch, c. 1906, from *Where Dorset Meets Devon*.

HORTON

Sturt's Folly

34

Map Ref
SU 032067

Most folly towers were built within the estate of a country mansion, either to enhance the view from the house or to command views stretching across the landowner's domain. The tower at Horton is an exception, for it stands starkly on a low hill in the middle of open fields and is not attached to any country house.

It was built in about 1765 by a local hunting squire, Humphrey Sturt, so that he could follow the hunt and watch the hounds work when he was no longer able to ride – or that is the story!

There is nothing beautiful about this sombre, seven-storeyed, six-sided, redbrick tower, with its three round, domed towers built to fourth-floor level on alternate corners. Its austere presence dominates rather than enhances the landscape.

An attractive view of Sturt's Folly.

HORTON HEATH

Monmouth's Ash

On 11 June 1685 the Duke of Monmouth, the illegitimate son of Charles II by his mistress, Lucy Walters, landed with great expectations on the sands west of the Cobb at Lyme Regis, to claim the throne of England from his uncle, James II. He marched to Taunton where he

Monmouth's ash
with, inset, the
plaque. (Margaret
Livingston)

proclaimed himself king, but the support he expected was not forthcoming and, with his largely un-trained and ill-equipped army, he was defeated at Weston Zoyland, on Sedgemoor, on 6 July.

He fled south through Dorset and two days later was captured, cowering and wet, in a ditch under an ash tree on the bleak, rolling wastes of Horton Heath. So his brief 27-day adventure, which had started with such high hopes in Dorset, ended in the same county with ignominy.

His capture there is commemorated by a metal plaque affixed to an ash, over which the bark has begun to grow; the present ash is a scion growing up from the stool of a much older tree which could well be the original ash. The plaque reads: 'After the Battle of Sedgemoor the Duke of Monmouth lay hidden beneath this tree and was found and taken prisoner by Sir William Portman and his Militia.'

Lyme Regis also commemorated Monmouth by naming the beach where he landed and a street after him, but that was well after the event!

The ditch and hedge surrounding the tree divides cultivated fields, and there is no evidence of a right of way to reach it.

ISLE OF PORTLAND

36

Map Ref
SY 676712

The 'Bill' and its Lighthouses

Mention Portland today and the word 'stone' springs to mind, but another word was associated with it 100 years ago – convicts. The stone is still there and quarried but the convicts, many of whom by hard labour had helped to quarry it, have gone. Gone too are the wagonettes and charabancs whose proprietors used to advertise excursions to Portland from Weymouth '. . . to have tea and see the convicts'!

Today the visitors come to look at the wild cliffs whose precipitous faces were worked for stone down to the shoreline and to see Portland's main attractions – its lighthouses.

The High Light (the westerly short one) and the Low Light (the easterly tall one) were built by Trinity House in 1716 to warn shipping to steer clear of the notorious graveyard of ships, the vicious current off the Bill – Portland Race. The Low Light was rebuilt in 1788 and then, in 1869, both the Low Light and the High Light were re-modelled and continued to operate until the present 135 ft high lighthouse was commissioned in 1906, much further out towards the end of the Bill. A plaque from the old 1788 Low Light was transferred to the present lighthouse and reads: 'For the Direction and Comfort of NAVIGATORS; for the Benefit and Security of COMMERCE and for a lasting Memorial of BRITISH HOSPITALITY to all Nations.'

The present light is now fully automated and is open to the public; the Low Light is a migratory bird observatory and the High Light is a guesthouse. Where else in Britain can one see three lighthouses all within half a mile of each other?

Convicts working in a Portland quarry, 1920s.

The Portland lighthouse of 1906 today.

KIMMERIDGE

A Nodding Donkey

37

Map Ref
SY 904793

At Kimmeridge there is a sight that would be more at home on the American plains – a nodding donkey, as the beam pump, quietly and rhythmically rising and falling, is called. For years oil shale was quarried and mined here, which when heated in retorts produced naphtha, paraffin wax and lubricating grease. It was exported world-wide and there were plans for vast quantities to be sent to France, and when processed to light the streets of Paris! The oil produced now comes from much deeper down and this donkey is the only one working commercially on the British mainland.

The nodding donkey at Kimmeridge. *(Peter Stanier)*

38

Map Ref
SY 909766

KIMMERIDGE

The Clavel Tower

In 1820, three years after inheriting the Smedmore house and estate, the Revd John Richard (having changed his name to Clavell, the family one) built this tower, which for some obscure reason has always been spelt with one 'l'. From this lonely viewpoint, perched on Hen Cliff above Kimmeridge Bay, the reclusive John Clavell could enjoy the sea views and air sitting out under the colonnaded veranda and in the cooler months in one of the three circular rooms, each with a fireplace.

Today the tower is in a sad condition, dilapidated and in such imminent danger of collapsing over the advancing cliff that the Landmark Trust has appealed for funds to move this Grade II* listed building back from the edge.

Clavel Tower at Kimmeridge.
(Peter Stanier)

KING'S STAG

An odd name for a village but one that conceals a romantic history. When King Henry III (1216–72) was out hunting in the Blackmore Forest, his hounds caught up with a stag that was crossing a little river. It was a pure white hart and the King was so taken with its beauty that the hounds were called off; the King decreed that it should be forever spared. However, during a chase in the forest Thomas de la Lynd, 'a gentleman with a fair estate in the County of Dorset', killed this white hart which greatly angered the King; a 'mulet' (a fine) was imposed forthwith for allowing this to happen, not only on Thomas, but the whole of the county where the hart roamed. This fine was called 'White Hart Silver' and had to be paid yearly into the Exchequer. There is, however, another version to this story: that the King had only wanted the stag for his own chase, but in that case why did he call off his hounds the first time?

Some 300 years later this 'tax' was still being levied, which so infuriated the Vicar of Broadwindsor, the Revd Thomas Fuller, that he complained bitterly, saying 'myself had paid a share for the sauce, who never tasted any of the meat; so it seems the King's Venison is sooner eaten than digested!' It must have been doubly annoying for him as, unusual in that day and age, Fuller was a vegetarian 'eating no meat' and did not agree with many sports, saying 'though Brute Beasts are made to be destroyed they are not made to be tormented'.

A bridge was built over the little stream where the King saw the white hart, and it has since always been known as White Hart Bridge.

KINGSTON

Eldon's Seat

Down the valley from Encombe House below Swyre Head and perched on an eminence some 400 yards from the cliff edge is Eldon's Seat, from which there are panoramic views: east across Chapman's Pool to St Aldhelm's Head, west to Kimmeridge and Portland and inland to the downs above Encombe House.

It was the Earl of Eldon's favourite spot, for it was an easy walk from the house, and here he had a squared stone 'seat' placed so that he could sit, admire the view and most probably muse on his humble beginnings as John Scott in Newcastle to his becoming the Lord Chancellor of England. Beside the track leading from the main entrance gates of the house to Swyre Head, which overlooks the

Eldon's Seat.

house and estate, are two similar squared stone 'seats' at SY 936787 and SY 941789. When the Earl died in October 1838, aged eighty-seven, his eldest daughter, Lady Elizabeth Repton, had the seat enlarged and inscribed as a memorial to her father. He and his boyhood sweetheart, Bessie, whom he married when he was twenty-one, lie in the old church at Kingston.

Touchingly, some 12ft down the slope to the east of Eldon's Seat is a low stone memorial (or grave?) to the Earl's favourite dog, a German spaniel called Pincher, who died two years later in October 1840. No doubt, being in the shade, it was where Pincher would lie while his master rested.

Pincher's memorial.

KNOWLTON

The Church in the Henge

Nothing can exemplify the taking over of one religion by another more clearly than this Norman church built exactly in the centre of a Neolithic henge mound of about 2,500 BC. The circular henge, with its double ditch and bank, is the most complete of numerous other earthworks and barrows in the vicinity. The church, with its twelfth-century nave and chancel and squat, flint-banded fourteenth-century tower, became disused in the eighteenth century when the roof fell in. The village, which straggled beside the nearby River Allen, was wiped out by the Black Death in about 1348; was this taken as a punishment for being sacrilegious, either by the old Gods or the new?

The site, under the guardianship of English Heritage, is now isolated amid the wide open fields and leaves a strong feeling of things unknown and unexplained.

The church in the henge.

LAMBERT'S CASTLE

The Tic-tac Men

Together with Pilsdon Pen, Lewesdon Hill and Coney's Castle, Lambert's Castle (840ft) is one of four prominent hill-forts built on the boundary between two Iron Age tribes – the Dumnonii of Devon and the Durotriges of Dorset – but who built which is open to question, as is who was Lambert. In 1709, in the reign of Queen Anne, a grant was given to hold an annual fair at Lambert's Castle on the Wednesday before the Feast of St John the Baptist (24 June). Gypsies coming to sell their horses looked upon it as an occasion for families to meet once a year, with the fair gradually becoming less important; in its place it became the venue for a yearly horse-race meeting and this continued until 1947 when, because of nobbling and fixing, the bookies (tic-tac men) would no longer attend.

In 1806, at the height of the scare caused by Napoleon's plans to invade England, the Admiralty in London needed to be in quick communication with Plymouth. A chain of visual telegraph stations was set up on high points linking the two. One was on Lambert's Castle with Stockland Hill to the west and Toller Down to the east. Each station consisted of a small house or hut, manned by an officer and two men, with six shutters erected on the roof that were operated as follows: the six shutters were in two blocks of three, set side by side, painted white with a black circle in the centre of each. These were worked by ropes within the building, each letter of the alphabet having its own sequence of open and closed shutters. A continuous watch was kept through fixed telescopes to the adjacent stations, and it was said that a message could be sent from Plymouth to London and a reply received in 20 minutes! Because of damage to the shutters in high winds the system was replaced by semaphore arms in 1816. Of course, neither system (invented by Lord George Murray and Sir Horace Popham respectively) could operate in adverse weather or at night, and in 1828 this line was abandoned.

Admiralty signal station, *c.* 1820, as it would have been on Lambert's Castle.

LODERS

Epitaph to a Blacksmith

This inscription was on a headstone in the graveyard at Loders, and could only have been thought up by the grave's humorous occupant, a blacksmith named Cox who died in 1823. Unfortunately in the ninety years since it was recorded, time and weather have taken their toll, and today it cannot be located, having probably been moved to make grass cutting easier.

> My sledge and hammer lie reclined
> My bellows too have lost their wind;
> My fire's extinct, my forge decayed
> And in the dust my vice is laid:
> My coal is spent, my iron's gone,
> My nails are driven. My work is done.

This slightly sardonic outlook on life and death was widespread during the eighteenth and early nineteenth centuries. There are similar sentiments expressed on headstones throughout the country and, perhaps because the allusions are apt, for blacksmiths in particular.

LYME REGIS

The Lyme Billies and their Viaduct

When the railway eventually came to Lyme Regis in 1903 the station was not only nearly a mile from the beaches but trippers had to toil up a 300ft hill to get back to it! It was, however, a wonder, in every sense of the word, that the railway reached Lyme at all. Firstly there was a thirty-year argument about where the branch was to start, at Chard Junction or Axminster; when Axminster was chosen the line had to climb some 500ft in its first 5 miles, necessitating many acute curves. Then once the top was reached another obstacle lay ahead – the deep valley at Cannington Farm which the line had to cross on a 93ft high, ten-arched concrete viaduct (in Devon – just – but very much part of the whole story). When the line was completed, because of all those acute curves, only the Adams 4–4–2 radial tank engines could negotiate them. The three engines used became affectionately known as

Cannington
Viaduct, 1920s.

Lyme Billies because of the well-known proclivity of billy-goats to climb to the top of everything! The line was built by the Axminster & Lyme Regis Light Railway Company, was taken over by the London & South-Western Railway in 1907 and closed in 1967, although the viaduct still stands as a magnificent memorial to the Railway Age.

LYME REGIS

Belmont and Eleanor Coade

Eleanor Coade (1733–1821) is one of the West Country's most eminent, if little-known daughters. She was born in Exeter but lived and worked at Lambeth in London, where she had her studios and factory. Here she employed artists to mould statues and building

The doorway at Belmont with Coade stone ornamentation.

ornamentations; these were then cast in 'Coade stone', a highly weather-resistant, ceramic stoneware (to her own secret formula) fired in a kiln. The superb statuary and decorations that she produced were used by all the leading architects and builders of the day, from Sir John Soane to Robert Adam, and these can be seen in most of the country's great houses and throughout London.

Mrs Coade (the Mrs was an honorary title Eleanor gave herself to help her as a business-woman) had known Lyme from childhood, for she had uncles living there; four of them in fact: George, George Jnr, Robert and John, all of them having been Mayor of Lyme between 1729 and 1780. In 1784 her uncle John, a merchant and manufacturer of serges, died and left her his house, Belmont, at the top of Pound Street, on the corner where the road goes down to the Cobb.

The 'Coade stone' monument to King George III at Weymouth.

It became Eleanor's summer home and she had it elaborately decorated with her 'Coade stone'. Urns surmount the balustrade around the roof, there are enriched string-courses and vermiculated quoins and surrounds to the round-headed ground floor windows and doorway. Masks are on the keystones (possibly Neptune over the door) with dolphins on the impost blocks – the only known occasion where Eleanor used dolphins as decorations. It was a superb advertisement for her stone products and still remains an architectural gem. Another extremely grand example of her work in 'Coade stone' can be seen in Dorset: the elaborately painted statue of King George III that dominates the southern end of Weymouth's Esplanade.

LYME REGIS

The Lepers' Well

On the steep hillside above the well a house of Carmelite friars (White Friars, so called because of the colour of their habits) of the Order of the Blessed Virgin Mary of Mount Carmel, was founded in about 1246. They were allowed 'to build "de novo" an oratory and houses for the inhabitants for ever'. It was also '. . . not to the King's prejudice if he granted William Dacre to give a messuage and eight acres of land here to the friars of that order . . . which premises were held of the King "in capite" as parcel of his farm at Lyme by service of paying yearly to him for the said farm 15s 10d'. White Friars were mendicants and, with little or no endowments of land, were dependent upon alms. The lepers' hospital would have been built around the pure well – it would not necessarily have had curative properties – and there would have been a small place of worship for the lepers. In 1336 a lepers' chapel was dedicated to 'The Blessed Virgin and Holy Spirit', but even by 1383 this must have fallen into disrepair for the Pope was granting 'indulgences' to those who contributed alms for the repair of the fabric and bell-tower. The well can be reached by walking along the Lynch, as the path is called between the mill stream and the chasm that is the River Lim, then crossing the river by a little footbridge. By the eighteenth century the whole site had become the garden of the great house in Broad Street, where Lord Chatham and his son William Pitt stayed as a boy of fourteen.

The lepers' well.

47

Map Ref
SY 335920

LYME REGIS

The Umbrella House

This delightful little polygonal 'cottage orné' has a central chimney, with its thatched roof coming down umbrella-like to the wooden veranda posts. The two posts, on either side of the heavily carved oak front door, have fretted capitals, and there is a diamond-shaped window over the doorway. It has been suggested that because of its roadside position it might once have been a toll-house of the Lyme

The Umbrella
House at Lyme.

Regis and Crewkerne Turnpike Trust; this, however, had been established in about 1758, well before this 'cottage orné'-style of architecture became popular between 1800 and 1830. It was much more likely to have been a lodge for some larger house, such as a similar but much larger two-storeyed lodge built in about 1810, attached to Gaunts House at Hinton Martell, also in Dorset. This theory is supported by there being two coats of arms on the wall of the Umbrella House – a shield divided by a chevron containing three birds (?), the details of which are difficult to make out. Could these be the coat of arms of the Coade family, prosperous merchants and serge-makers of the town, who provided several mayors during the eighteenth century? Their coat of arms was a shield divided by a chevron containing three coots, and only a few hundred yards down the road was one of their homes, Belmont. The Umbrella House has recently been extended at the back, but in such a sympathetic manner as to leave one wondering if it had not always been like that.

The lodge to Gaunt's House.

48

Map Ref
SY 344922

LYME REGIS

Bridging the Buddle

The twelfth-century bridge over the Buddle, as the River Lim is called where it nears its mouth, had several small arches, with its replacement 200 years later having only one arch. This was necessary to prevent flooding at high tide, when the flow of the river was held back; in fact, the actual bed of the river had later to be lowered to prevent flooding farther upstream. What makes this bridge especially interesting is that, certainly in the eighteenth and nineteenth centuries, the south side of the bridge could not have been seen from the north side of the road. It would have appeared simply as a narrow little street of rather mean houses contiguous with each other. Two of

The south side of the bridge from Broad Street, *c.* 1907.

the houses were in fact actually built over the river and abutting the street, although, as can be seen in old illustrations, they were built of timber not brick or stone. One of these was occupied for a time by Mary Anning and her family. Old London Bridge had been lined with shops and houses on both sides while Pulteney Bridge, over the River Avon at Bath, is still, to all intents and purposes, a shopping street. This unique feature survived at Lyme until 1913 when the road was widened, with a masonry widening of the bridge's southern side. Even now, looking over the bridge parapet with a gale coming in from the south-east on a high tide, the view is awesome; what it must have been like living over it in an insubstantial house beggars the imagination!

The old bridge from the beach, *c.* 1905.

LYME REGIS

An Old Wooden Letter Box

Before the advent of the first pre-paid postage stamp in 1840 – the Penny Black – there had been two procedures for sending letters. They could be taken to the Posting House (post office), handed over the counter to the post master who would assess the cost, depending on the distance the letter had to go; or they could be 'posted' with the recipient paying the cost. An instruction to all Letter Receivers (Post Masters) dated 1 May 1814 stated: 'Every Office or Receiving-House must have a Letter Box in the front for unpaid letters. It must be fixed to a point convenient for Public access, be large and strong, and (if of iron) be kept locked, with the key out, till the proper time of emptying for each dispatch. The words Unpaid Letter Box to be painted on it. . . .' Until 1853, when the post office introduced the iron pillar and wall boxes, it had been up to the local post master to devise his own. Some were of iron with a lockable door, some replaced a shop window pane and others, as in this example in Norman House, Combe Street, Lyme Regis, were let into the wall of the office beside a window, the letters falling directly into the office.

The wooden letter-box in Combe Street.

Norman House is believed to have been Lyme's 'Posting House' from 1799 until 1853, when the post office moved to Broad Street. Posting 'slots' were usually horizontal, but in 1846 the post office recommended vertical slots; this they thought would make the theft of letters more difficult, but the idea was abandoned in 1856. This rare wooden example with horizontal slots, one being later adapted to a vertical slot (only possible with a wooden box) was uncovered when the cement rendering on the house was removed, which, of course, is what had saved it for all these years. It is now listed. A very rare octagonal cast-iron pillar box with a vertical slot, made in 1853, is still in use in Dorset, at Barnes Cross, near Bishops Caudle (ST 693117). The provision of vertical letter-boxes in the doors of private houses persisted for many years and some are still in use today.

Cast-iron, vertical-slotted box near Bishops Caudle, the oldest in use in the country.

LYME REGIS

Sherborne Lane

Picturesque Sherborne Lane, the narrow and very steep way leading down from the top of Broad Street to the River Lim, is a reminder of a one-time Lyme 'industry'; pan-dried sea salt was once a vital commodity, its use the only way many foodstuffs could be preserved. Because of its importance the making of salt was often in the hands of the powerful monasteries and abbeys. In 774 Gynewulf, the West Saxon King, gave the monks of Sherborne Abbey 'the land of one manor near the west bank of the River Lim, and not far from the place where it falls into the sea, so that salt for the said Church may be boiled there for supplying various wants'. This salt trade continued for many centuries, with the abbey charging a toll on all that was sold as surplus to their requirements. The Domesday Survey of 1086 showed no fewer than twenty-six 'saltmen' working in Lyme. The steepness and narrowness of Sherborne Lane would have been no obstacle to the transportation of the salt as it was carried on pack-horses, in panniers, or dorsers, as they were called in Dorset. Throughout the West Country the narrow, hump-backed packhorse bridges can still be seen to one side of what was once a ford; these were essential in the transportation of wool and salt, for neither could be allowed to get wet. There is a splendid (restored) medieval packhorse bridge and ford (when the stream is high) at Okeford Fitzpaine (ST 772101).

'Hydromania! or a Touch of the Sub Lyme and Beautiful . . . The Beach at Lyme Regis'. George Cruikshank (1792–1878) drew the bathing machines and the 'bathing belles' on to an original 1819 sketch of the Cobb by 'The Amateur' and also gave it its satirical caption, neither of which were appreciated by the good people of Lyme! 'The Amateur' was the pseudonym under which the author of all those naval and adventure stories, Captain Marryat, sketched and painted. Cruikshank's association with Lyme Regis is not known, but Captain Marryat would have known the area as one of his daughters, Emilia, married Mr H.E. Norris, a Charmouth surgeon.

Packhorse bridge and ford at Fivehead Neville.

LYME REGIS

A Volcano on the Cliffs

At the beginning of January 1908 there was a large fall of material from the second tier of the cliff on the Spittles, near Black Ven and about a mile east of Lyme. On the 19th of that month clouds of sulphurous smoke began to be emitted from the mound, gradually intensifying until it became 'volcano-like' in appearance. This phenomenon caused great excitement and interest, with visitors flocking to view the 'volcano', so that the railway did exceptionally good business! It was not, of course, volcanic in origin, but the spontaneous combustion, after heavy rains, of the bituminous shale, iron pyrites and cement rocks from the beds which included 'fire-stone nodules'. The spectacle continued until June when the mound split in two, exposing an interior 'very like a brick kiln, from the baked condition of the stone'. This was not the first time such an event had occurred, for a visitor writing in 1817 observed '. . . there is very much bituminous matter in the soil, which has often taken fire after heavy rains, and produced, at a distance, the appearance of large flames, but at a nearer approach, smoke alone was perceived'. In October 2001, nearly 100 years after the outbreak of 1908 and after many movements of the cliffs above Black Ven, the sea uncovered slag-like material and glazed burnt stone from the base of the cliff. This material clearly showed the great heat that must have been generated all those years ago.

The volcano on the cliff, 1908.

MAPPERTON

The Posey Tree and the Death of a Village

Standing forlornly in a little triangle of rough grass where a track meets the Mapperton to Melplash Lane is the massive dead trunk of a sycamore tree. It bears a small plaque with its name - posey tree – and a brief outline of its history. The story goes back to 1666 with a terrible outbreak of bubonic plague afflicting the area. The population

52

Map Ref
SY 496996

All that remains of
the posey tree.

of Mapperton, then a sizable hamlet, was decimated, with those remaining having to bury over eighty dead. Because of the unsuitability of the soil surrounding their church, All Saints', the village had no graveyard, and it had always been the tradition of the villagers of Mapperton to bury their dead in the churchyard at Netherbury, some 3 miles away. On this occasion the people of Netherbury, who had so far escaped the disease, objected to the corpses of those who had died of the plague being brought into their parish and proceeded to the track junction to stop them coming any further, carrying, of course, posies of flowers and herbs to ward off any contagion. Whether or not they were stopped by force or by persuasion, the poor souls of Mapperton must have been out-numbered and too weak to resist. They went instead to the slopes of Warren Hill where they dug a pit as a communal grave in which to bury their dead – not in consecrated ground but within sight of Netherbury church.

Mapperton never recovered; many holdings reverted, untenanted, to the manor, dwellings fell into disrepair and collapsed, and even today there is no village, only the beautiful manor-house, the church and a few scattered farms and houses.

How old was the tree? Even a well-tended sycamore has only a life of about 200 years, so this tree was either planted in remembrance well after the event or it is a replacement for an earlier tree. Will another be planted now? The garden at Mapperton House, established mainly in the 1920s, is open to the public during the summer and one of the most delightful in Dorset.

MAPPOWDER

The Blackamoor Busts

The last mansion of the Coker family at Mappowder, built in 1664, was demolished in the eighteenth century, with a farmhouse being built on the site, obviously using much of the original material from the mansion. The gateway to the mansion had massive, dressed-stone pillars, which have survived, and are now the entrance to the farmhouse. Each pillar is surmounted by the bust, most unusually, of a Negro, or as they were then referred to, a Blackamoor. The significance of these busts is open to speculation; with a play on the name Blackamoor, do they allude to the site being in the Vale of Blackmore, or to the fact that the Cokers were involved with and made money from the slave trade?

Across the lane from these pillars is the entrance to the old farm buildings, which also has stone gateposts, one of which is surmounted by a four-sided sundial. This possibly came from the mansion's garden, as it is unlikely to have been made specially for a farm gateway. The gnomons have all nearly rusted away, but of course the one on the north face would have been simply ornamental in order to preserve the symmetry.

The Blackamoor busts at Mappowder.

54

Map Ref
ST 734058

MAPPOWDER

Topiary Run Riot

Many grand houses in Dorset have fine topiary in their gardens, but this example at Mappowder, seen briefly in passing this year, takes some beating.

Completely dominating the cottage, it is as large as the garden itself and one can only guess how long it took to reach this size! It could represent a house, a hat or perhaps it just evolved; there is, however, a corresponding hole on the other side.

A tree at Mappowder.

MELBURY BUBB

The Upside-down Font

55

Map Ref
ST 596065

From Hell Corner a lane leads westwards to the foot of wooded Bubb Down, but it goes no further than an old manor-house and the little church of St Mary the Virgin, for the parish consists of no more than a few scattered farms and houses.

The name Bubb is derived from a Saxon called Bubba who lived hereabouts and the church retains one relic from that period – its font. Thought to have originally been the base of an eleventh-century cross, it was, possibly because of its shape, turned upside-down and hollowed out to be used as a font by the Normans. The font is elaborately carved with animals and they too are now inverted.

But could the 'cross' have been turned upside-down deliberately, because it depicted a carved bestiary? The Anglo-Saxons incorporated many religious symbols and customs from earlier, and less Christian, beliefs, and these carvings might well have been regarded as pagan by the more devout Normans. It might even be that, loath to waste a good piece of carved stone, they turned it upside down to sanctify its pagan origins.

The upside-down font with its bestiary at Melbury Bubb.

The carving around the font depicts four large animals: 'a stag biting a serpent whose coils interlace the feet of the other animals; a tall horse with paws not hooves; a lion with a mane biting a small dog with its tail between its legs; and a large animal with a mane facing the horse. There are two small two-legged dragons between the larger animals.' There is nothing Christian in any of that!

About 10 miles to the east, in the church of St Peter and St Paul at Mappowder, there is another reminder of how the old beliefs clung on in the countryside; carved on a capital in the chancel is a 'green man' complete with foliage sprouting from his nostrils!

The 'green man' in the church of St Peter and St Paul in Mappowder.

MILTON ABBAS

The Turf Steps

56

Map Ref
ST 800023

When, in 1786, Joseph Damer, later 1st Earl of Dorchester, decided to build his grand new house at Milton, close by the Abbey Church, only one thing spoilt his view – the little town of Milton! So he had its 100-odd houses, grammar school, brewery, inns and the old abbey buildings (with the exception of the Abbey Church) pulled down, and had a new village built out of sight a mile away in a secluded valley. It had a new school, church, almshouses and forty identical semi-detached thatched cottages, twenty on each side of a broad street, with long gardens stretching up the hillsides behind them. Not all the original inhabitants of the town were rehoused and Damer, by one means or another, got rid of the rest. The cottages were undoubtedly superior to those in the old town, for Fanny Burney, novelist and friend of Dr Johnson, thought that 'they were too good for the Poor'. Today it must be the most photographed village in Dorset, if not the whole country.

However, the most extraordinary thing that Damer built was in his own garden on the site of the old town. Directly to the east of the Abbey Church, standing on a low ridge, is St Catherine's Chapel, which was originally built by King Athelstan in about AD 925.

Milton Abbas street, *c.* 1935. It is much busier now!

Damer had a flight of 111 steps constructed from his garden up to the chapel, but uniquely (probably in the world) these are green turf steps, bordered by yew hedges, surviving to the present day through the care of successive gardeners and the fact that few people used them. They are not allowed to be used now, but they can be viewed.

The turf steps at Milton Abbey.

MORETON

The Clear Glass-Engraved Windows

In October 1940 the little church of St Nicholas at Moreton was severely damaged by a German bomb; the north wall was blown out, the interior devastated and the stained-glass windows shattered. It was not until 1950 that the church was rededicated and a courageous decision taken to replace the windows with clear glass, to be engraved by the foremost glass engraver in Britain, Laurence Whistler, who lived at Lyme Regis.

The five apse windows were the first to be completed in 1955, and because the church is dedicated to St Nicholas, patron saint of children and Christmas, they are a celebration of light and festivity. One of the windows on the north, or winter, side of the apse shows a Christmas tree, and one on the south an ash tree, ancient symbol of happiness. Others depict the dove, the passion and the sacrament and the metaphorical 'true vine' of Christ hangs from the Cross.

Over the next twenty years these were added to as each commemorative occasion arose or a donor came forward. From the beginning light, physical and spiritual, was Laurence Whistler's theme – images of candlelight, sunlight, jewel-light, star-light and lightning – with a gradual change in his style, from structure in execution and content to freedom of form. The vestry window shows a storm, the lightning taking the shape of the nearby Rivers Frome and Piddle with a fire-ball showing the position of the church, while the west window is a spiral galaxy of stars.

This beautiful, exquisite work makes the little church unique, for it is the only one in the world to have clear glass engraved windows.

Detail from the Seasons Window – summer – by Laurence Whistler, at St Nicholas' Church at Moreton. (Moreton Parochial Church Council)

58

Map Ref
SY 660822

NOTTINGTON

The Spa

The existence of a curative spring was first mentioned in 1719, when it formed a large pond; in 1750 a Dr Archer had a low circular wall, or 'collar', built around the spring itself to prevent it being fouled by animals. The water issuing from the spring was said to smell noxious and when it was subsequently analysed was found to contain free hydrogen sulphate – but in those days anything which smelt or tasted awful must be good!

In 1832, with Weymouth becoming popular as a watering-place for the health conscious and only an easy 3 miles away, Thomas Shore built the three-storeyed bathhouse enclosing the spring which provided 'capacious warm vapour and shower baths in addition to drinking facilities, and there were connected lodging apartments'. It was open from 8 a.m. to 8 p.m. and the charges were:

Cold: Marble bath, 2s; Shower bath, 1s; Shower bath with feet in warm water, 1s 6d; Jet d'eau, 1s 6d.
Warm: Vapour bath, 3s; Jet d'eau, 1s 6d.
Child's (under 12 years): 3 in bath, 3s 6d; 4 in bath, 4s; Attendant 6d.

Nottington spa house as it is today.

At the start cures were claimed for cancer, rickets, rheumatism, scurvy and diabetes. However, the treatment was said to be beneficial for skin diseases and, when taken internally, for clearing the blood, improving digestion, clearing worms from the intestines and toning the nervous system.

With advances in medical knowledge and changing social mores, the spa closed in about 1900, to be replaced by a laundry until 1911 when it became a private house.

OSMINGTON

Ride a White Horse

Paying a highly visible tribute to King George III's many visits to Weymouth, 'to take sea bathing', is a figure of the King riding a horse which is cut into the chalk of the downland above Osmington. As the *Universal Magazine* reported in 1808:

> an equestrian figure of His Majesty has lately been formed in the chalk on Osmington Hill, opposite the Bay of Weymouth. Although the length is 280 feet and the height 223 feet, yet the likeness to the King is well preserved and the symmetry of the horse is complete. It has been carried into effect under the direction of Mr Wood, bookseller, at the particular request and expense of John Ranier Esq., brother of the late Admiral.

It is said that it did not meet with the King's approval as it depicted him riding away from Weymouth. But by then the King was not quite himself!

King George III rides away from Weymouth.

60

Map Ref
SY 705996

PIDDLETRENTHIDE

The Piddle Inn

The village name originated with its 30 hides of land (a hide being approximately 80 acres) that lay beside the little River Piddle, one of the many villages with the name Piddle or Puddle incorporated into them. Over the years the name has given rise to ribald country humour with the local public house becoming the Piddle Inn. Until quite recently the entrepreneurial landlord had miniature china chamber-pots made, and these became prized possessions for locals and visitors alike as mementoes of drinking there, but of little practical use! No longer available, they are now rare curiosities.

As one can see, it can't hold much!

61

Map Ref
SY 612875

PORTISHAM

The Hardy Monument

Perched 770ft up on Black Down, looking out over the vast sweep of Thomas Hardy's Dorset, from his Casterbridge (Dorchester) to Budmouth (Weymouth) and the Isle of Slingers (Portland) is the massive, octagonal 70ft Hardy Monument. But wait a minute! That is the wrong Thomas Hardy, as so many visitors discover to their surprise. This monument, with its wide views over the English Channel, is to commemorate Admiral Sir Thomas Masterman Hardy, Bart, CCB (1769–1839), Nelson's close friend and Flag Captain under him on the *Victory* at Trafalgar. Hardy was born at Kingston Russell, a bare 3 miles away down the Bride Valley, and when he was nine his family moved to Portisham; he remained a true 'local', always favouring Dorset food – sea 'cale' (a Dorset delicacy), Dorset mutton, Dorset 'Blue Vinny' cheese and Dorset beer, which he described 'as the best ever drunk'. He became Vice-Admiral, commanding home and American waters, and Governor of Greenwich Hospital, where he is buried. It is sad that he should be most remembered for Nelson's reputed last words 'Kiss me, Hardy' (said in affection only), when Nelson's actual last words were 'God bless you, Hardy'.

This supremely ugly monument was designed by A.D. Troyte and built in 1844. It has been variously described as looking like a chess-piece, a pepper pot and, most unkindly, as a 'factory chimney with a crinoline around its feet'! In truth, it is not unlike the edifice on Kitt Hill, in Cornwall, which really is a chimney!

The Hardy
Monument.

62

Map Ref
SY 602858

PORTISHAM

By a Wall Divided

Against the outside of the south wall of St Peter's Church at Portisham, is the tomb of William Weare and on the wall itself is a tablet, recently restored, with his epitaph, which reads:

> William Weare lies here in dust
> As thou and I and all men must.
> Once plundered by Sabean* force
> Some cald it war but others worse.
> With confidence he pleads his cause
> And Kings to be above those laws.
> September Eyhth Day died hee
> When near the Date of 63
> Ano Domini 1670.

It is said that he wanted to be buried 'neither in the church nor outside', so he lies in the wall, certainly carrying his bitterness over his treatment to his grave (his property had been sequestrated by the Parliamentarians as he was a Royalist).

On the wall of the south aisle inside the church, exactly opposite William's, is a table with an epitaph to Mary Weare, wife of Robert Weare and William's sister-in-law. This reads:

> Underneath lies her whose actions pend
> The perfect copie of a friend,
> Whose good meek heart did always shun
> Such things as ought not to be done.
> Rest then for ever, rest alone,
> Thy ashes can be touched by none.
> Mary wife of Robert Weare Deceased the
> 26 Day of October anno Domini 1675.

These words have always been taken as praise for an ideal wife, yet there must be some reason the two tablets should so exactly back on to each other as well as being buried in such close proximity, yet with a wall between them. Perhaps the clue lies in the enigmatic words of Mary's epitaph; did she also suffer at the hands of the 'Sabean force', or did she have unrequited feelings towards her brother-in-law, or he to her? We shall never know. It is significant that there are no monuments to either William's wife (if he had one) or to Mary's husband, Robert.

* In the Book of Job: 1.15, the Sabeans were an Arabian tribe who stole Job's cattle.

The tomb of
William Weare
outside St Peter's
Church at
Portisham.

POXWELL

63

Map Ref
SY 741841

A Fountain of Life

During the nineteenth century many landowners learnt that the old wells used by their tenants and others in the villages could easily be contaminated by cesspits, middens and such like, causing water-borne diseases, such as cholera. To prevent this, many of the more public-spirited landowners provided a piped supply of pure water from a small reservoir or spring.

Beside the road at Poxwell is an elaborate stone surround to an iron spout, from which pure water, fed by a spring, would have flowed continuously. Above the spout an almost feudal inscription reads: 'This conduit was erected by Richard T. Richard Esq. for the use of the poor of his parish of Poxwell. 1843.' The name Poxwell

The spout at Poxwell.

suggests that the original well was either polluted, giving the pox, or had curative properties. The latter must be the case for the old name for the well was 'Puck's [Fairy's] Well'.

This altruism continued throughout the nineteenth century with a very late example in Thorncombe. Here the supply was to roadside taps in the village with an elaborate water-standard in the centre (ST 375032). The inscription reads: 'This supply of drinking water for the people of Thorncombe was planned by William Herbert Evans of Forde Abbey in whose memory it is laid on. 1902.'

The memorial fountain at Thorncombe.

PUNCKNOWLE

64

Map Ref
SY 535877

The Spy House

To the south of Puncknowle a hill overlooks the whole panorama of the coast, westwards to Lyme Regis and Start Point and east over the sea to Portland. Today it is called The Knoll, but in the past it was known as Punnell Knob or Punnell Nose. On its very top is a tiny 'house' whose original purpose is shrouded in as much mystery as it often is now by the thick sea-mists which roll in hereabouts. There are many explanations as to its origin: it was a pleasure house or gazebo for a local landowner; it was a look-out used by the preventative men to curb smuggling which was once rife along this stretch of coast; or it was used as a watch-house during the wars with Napoleon in case of invasion. It became surrounded by trees, but these were blown down a few years ago together with the roof of the little house. The roof has now been replaced, although the house is doorless and windowless with nothing remaining inside. It is worth the steep walk up for the view.

The little house on Puncknowle Knoll.

SHAFTESBURY

The Byzant

65

Map Ref
ST 861229

Anyone who has visited Shaftesbury will know that the town sits on the top of a hill so, as any well had to be at least 120ft deep, water was always scarce. To ease this situation water was carried up from outside the borough from springs at Enmore Green; for this practice, however, a yearly tribute had to be paid to the Lord of the Manor of Gillingham, on whose land the springs were situated. Going in procession on the Sunday before Ascension Day, certainly from 1655 if not before, the Mayor had to take tributes of the local produce: ale, the best wheaten bread, a calf's head and a pair of gloves (a highly regarded present) together with the mysterious Byzant, which was described as 'like a May Garland with gold and peacock's feathers'. This was then given to the Mayor to take back to the town.

The Byzant in Shaftesbury Museum. *(Shaftesbury Historical Society)*

Some time later the ceremony was changed to the Monday following Ascension Day, when it became an occasion for civic pomp and jollity. The last couple to be married in the town that year each received a new outfit of clothes and were declared 'Lord and Lady' for the day. The Byzant also became more elaborate, hung with silver plate and jewels lent by the local worthies. In 1771, costing £17 11*s*, it became the gaudy object of gilded wood hung with decorations that can be seen in the town museum today. The origin of the name 'Byzant' was possibly a gold coin or tribute. The ceremony was discontinued following the installation of a pumped and piped water supply.

66

Map Ref
SY 637164

SHERBORNE

The Weighbridge House

On the north side of Half Moon Street in Sherborne, opposite the Abbey Church, is a small, semi-circular, brick structure with a stone roof, about 6ft high and 5ft wide and deep. Looking something like an extremely small lock-up, it is in fact to house the weighing mechanism for a weighbridge, built in the middle of the eighteenth century.

The compound lever platform weighbridge was invented in 1744 by the brilliant carpenter and inventor, John Wyatt, who worked in the Soho foundry, Birmingham, which belong to the great Matthew Boulton, of steam engine fame. Being installed so soon after it was invented, the weighbridge must have been an object of wonder, as well as of great convenience to traders and wagoners, for previously the only way in which any cart or wagon could be weighed was by a large and cumbersome form of steel-yard (a wooden arm pivoted at one end with a weight that could be moved along the length of the long arm).

This early mechanism was replaced by a more modern version in 1850 and, although the bridge itself was removed in 1950 for road widening, the little building still retains the arm and mechanism.

The weighbridge house at Sherborne.

SHERBORNE

The Conduit

At the bottom of Cheap Street in Sherborne, is a small, open-sided stone building, built in the tenth century in the cloisters of Sherborne Abbey as a washing house and laundry for the monks. At the Dissolution of the Monasteries in about 1539 it was moved to its present position to make a little market house. It has since had a chequered history becoming in turn a water supply, hence the name Conduit, a reading room, a police station, a 'penny bank' and now, finally, the open shelter it is today.

The Conduit at Sherborne.

68

STANTON ST GABRIEL

The Old Church

Standing isolated in a field 200ft above the sea and at the very foot of Golden Cap (619ft) are the ruins (now conserved) of the tiny church dedicated to St Gabriel. For 700 years it was the place of worship for a small community of farmers and fishermen who formed the parish of Stanton St Gabriel. Today there is only a farmhouse and a cottage (both holiday lets) near the green around which the tiny hamlet once clustered – although a circular sheep dip survives. It was last used in about 1800; in 1841 a new church to St Gabriel was built about a mile inland, in the more populous hamlet of Morcombelake, on the main road from Bridport to Charmouth. Fortunately it was built before the ornate High Victorian fashions came in, with simple white walls and dark roof rafters, and with the font and the severe, yet graceful, rood screen from the old church giving it a continuity with the past.

There is a long and flowery verse telling the story of the founding of the old church based, reputedly, on an 'old manuscript', the gist of which is as follows: a young man, Bertram, with his new bride, was on a barque crossing the English Channel when a violent storm arose and the vessel was about to founder. Bertram asked the master to let them have the one small boat so that they might have a chance of being saved. They prayed to St Gabriel for deliverance and swore that

The old church at St Gabriel, *c.* 1930.

should they survive they would build to his name. After three days the gale abated but Bertram's bride had succumbed to the elements. They eventually drifted ashore below Golden Cap and Bertram, true to his word, built a chapel to the glory of St Gabriel and buried his bride under the altar.

STINSFORD

His Heart Lies in Dorset

69
Map Ref
SY 712910

Thomas Hardy (1840–1928) was born, bred, lived and died in the Dorset he so loved and with its people, towns, villages and countryside woven into his novels and poetry. Although known as 'The Village Atheist', he had personally made arrangements with the Vicar of Stinsford regarding his burial there. However, after his death

Thomas Hardy's grave at Stinsford.

The small effigy of an unknown crusader in the church of St Peter and St Paul at Mappowder.

many thought his reputation as a nationally known writer warranted a grander resting place – none other than Poets' Corner in Westminster Abbey. His widow, Florence, was appalled but was overruled as to the actual grand funeral envisaged by his publisher, Macmillan, although in the end it turned into a complete shambles. His heart, however, was removed before cremation, and was buried at Stinsford, where he was born, safe in the soil of his beloved Dorset – truly 'The Return of the Native', for he had written 'I shall sleep quite calmly at Stinsford, whatever happens'.

In a niche in the south wall of the church of St Peter and St Paul in Mappowder, is an effigy of an unknown crusader in full armour, holding a heart against his breast. The effigy is only 1ft 9in long, and it is thought that when the knight died on a crusade only his heart was brought back to his home, hence the unusually small resting place.

STOKE ABBOTT

The Curfew Bell

Stoke Abbott must be one of the prettiest villages in Dorset and is steeped in history, albeit of a parochial nature.

It carries on the centuries-old custom of the curfew bell, rung every morning during the summer at 7 a.m. The villagers got a little peace during the Second World War when bells could only be rung to give warning of an imminent German invasion. The custom was revived when the war ended – although not at the same hour as previously – 5.30 a.m. summer and winter!

It was probably because of the strong spring that still gushes out of the hillside that the village grew up here. It would have been the focal point every day, when water would be fetched in buckets filled under a spout and horses brought to drink from the trough. For those without wells this continued until 1961 when piped water was at last brought to the area. The present horse-trough goes back to 21 May 1752 when Richard Symes 'Pd for the stone water trough for ye spring at Stoke £1 4s 0d'. The lion's head spout, which still has a chained metal drinking cup, looks old but was, in fact, a replacement for the original to commemorate Queen Elizabeth II's Coronation in 1953!

No doubt the spring water continues to be favoured by a few; some years ago, when there was a notice over the spout warning that it was 'Unfit to drink' (now removed), an old man with his bucket told me: 'I'm used to it!'

The horse-trough at Stoke Abbott.

71

Map Ref
SY 388931

STONEBARROW HILL

A Tragedy Remembered

Just inside a wood to the east of Stonebarrow Hill is a stone monument, surrounded by iron railings, which is inscribed:

> This stone marks the spot where Robert Henry Hildyard Esq. fell dead whilst out shooting September 8th 1876, aged 40. He was 2nd Secretary in H.M. Diplomatic Service, Lord of the Manor of Catherston and J.P. of the County. He was the only child of his mother and she is a widow. 'What should thou knowest not now but those shall know Hereafter. Enter not into Judgement with thy Servant O Lord for in thy sight no living shall be justified'. Let them who visit this spot day from their hearts make him to be numbered with thy Saints in Glory Everlasting.

A mother's memorial to her son on Stonebarrow Hill.

As the *Dorsetshire County Chronicle* reported, 'some time in the afternoon they were walking up the hill (towards Stonebarrow) when Mr. Hildyard made an attempt to sit down, but suddenly fell forward and expired . . .'. Mr H.E. Norris, the local surgeon, reported 'death by heart disease . . . and the coroner being satisfied, an inquest was deemed unnecessary'. Mr Hildyard is buried in a vault in the churchyard at Catherston Leweston.

When the monument was erected it was not surrounded with trees but on an open slope looking out over the sea. Today the area is owned by the National Trust and, although the monument is not signposted, a stile has been put in the field hedge now surrounding the wood.

STUDLAND

The Agglestone

On the top of a low knoll in the heathland behind Studland is the Agglestone, a massive lump of ferruginous sandstone, some 18ft high, 80ft round and estimated at weighing 500 tons, which has resisted erosion while the loose sands surrounding it have been swept away by the elements. Not quite as upright as it once was, but still a prominent landmark; there is a smaller version, the Puck Stone about a quarter of a mile away.

Any isolated feature has always collected a story or myth; the one about the Agglestone was put into doggerel by a John Webber in 1851:

> Here's the famous Agglestone
> Said to be by Satan thrown
> At Corfe Castle in the night
> From the neighbouring Isle of Wight.

Mr Webber does not say, however, what Satan was doing on the Isle of Wight – perhaps he was practising for his more successful hurling at Portlock, in Somerset!

The Agglestone, c. 1905.

The ruins of Corfe Castle from the west: not the result of a more successful throw by the Devil, but the use of hundreds of tons of gunpowder when the castle was 'slighted' by the Parliamentarians in 1645.

STURMINSTER NEWTON

Fiddleford Manor

73

Map Ref
ST 801136

This gem of a small country manor-house was built in the fourteenth century for William Latimer, Sheriff of Somerset and Dorset, but was enlarged and 'modernised' during the sixteenth century. There is a Great Hall and a Solar with undercroft, both open to the rafters, and what rafters they are! The fourteenth-century oak timbers are cusped and braced, with those in the Great Hall smoke-blackened by the central open fire it once had. Both Great Hall and Solar now have massive stone fireplaces with the Great Hall having a gallery.

The whole building, extremely plain from the outside, is a wonderful example of how the lesser gentry lived, as opposed to those living in the grand houses and castles. The building is owned by the Pitt-Rivers Estate but is under the stewardship of English Heritage, which has conserved and maintained it splendidly. Set idyllically on the banks of the River Stour, admission to the house is free and there is a small car park.

Looking up in the Solar at Fiddleford Manor.

SWANAGE

Little Bits of Old London

Much of the stone used in the new buildings erected in London during the nineteenth century came from the quarries of Purbeck and was shipped out of Swanage. One of the large contractors using the stone was John Mowlem (the construction firm of Mowlem is still one of the largest in England), who lived in Swanage although his headquarters were in London. Ships returning to Swanage did so mostly under ballast, using material from demolished buildings. So John Mowlem and his nephew George Burt, who succeeded him in the business when

The town hall.

he died in 1868, used selected items from this ballast to enhance Swanage. This has left the town with some decidedly quirky buildings and monuments which now greatly add to its charm.

The clock-tower, built to commemorate the Duke of Wellington, had been erected on the Surrey side of London Bridge, but had to be removed as it was causing traffic problems. Mowlem had it carefully taken down and re-erected as the Wellington clock tower, near the shore between the stone-loading pier and Peveril Point (SZ 038786). However, he couldn't get the clock itself, so the tower now has four round windows instead!

The town hall in the High Street (SZ 028787) was designed by the Weymouth architect Crickmay in traditional Victorian style in 1872. However, in 1883 a part of the ornate façade from Mercer's Hall, in Cheapside, built by Christopher Wren in 1670, was 'stuck on' to the town hall's front, making what was very ordinary, extraordinary.

The Wellington clock-tower.

A little further up the High Street is the house George Burt had built for himself in 1875 – Purbeck House, also designed by Crickmay. On a wall in a corner of its grounds sits a magnificent, octagonal gazebo which commands a view down the High Street. The walls of the house are built of large chips of coloured marble, left over when Mowlem was building the steps of the Albert Memorial, but with plain Purbeck stone edgings. In the courtyard a two-storeyed wing of the house is supported on an iron plate and cast-iron column from Billingsgate Market, and in the courtyard itself are stone bollards from Millbank Prison. Purbeck House is now an hotel.

On a grassy slope near the entrance to the new pier stand two massive Tuscan stone columns, complete with capitals, now making an imposing 'garden ornament'. For many years they were in the grounds of the Grosvenor Hotel (another of Burt's ventures) and were removed to their present position when the hotel was demolished

some years ago. Where Burt acquired them in London isn't known.

Scattered all over the town are other relics scavenged from the streets of London: lampposts and bollards, some having the inscriptions 'St. Anne's Soho' and 'St. Martin in the Fields' cast on to them, and a gatepost with 'City of London'. All in all, John Mowlem and particularly George Burt, who died in 1894, left Swanage a far richer place and a shining example of the present 'buzz word' – recycling!

The Tuscan columns.

Purbeck House.

SWANAGE

The Globe

Overlooking the sea at Durlston Head is George Burt's Globe, a feature which has proved fascinating for generations of visitors, but why he had it made is not recorded – was it educational, purely ornamental or an idiosyncratic whim?

The Globe, made from eight segments of Portland stone from Purbeck, is 10ft in diameter and weighs 40 tons. All the land masses of the world are shown and named as well as the lines of latitude and longitude. On surrounding slabs of stone details are engraved about the age and nature of the earth, the moon, the sun and the stars; there are passages from the Psalms and from Shakespeare and what was probably his philosophy of life: 'Let Justice be your guide to all your actions. Let Prudence direct you, Temptation chasten you and Fortitude support you.' Good Victorian values!

The Globe,
c. 1930.

76

Map Ref
SZ 033772

SWANAGE

Durlston Castle

When George Burt acquired the Durlston Estate he had high hopes of developing it into a superior suburb of Swanage, but his dream was never realised. In 1878 he did, however, build a restaurant on a superbly elevated site on Durlston Head, with broad views over the English Channel and his famous Globe (see **75**). It was designed by his usual architect, Crickmay, in a completely preposterous style and it was given an even more preposterous name – Durlston Castle. A few years later the eminent surgeon and author of *Highways and Byways of Dorset*, Sir Frederick Treves, wrote that 'it combines the architectural features of a refreshment buffet, a tram terminus and a Norman keep!'

It remained as a restaurant until recently and is to become the heritage centre for the 'Eastern Gateway to the Jurassic Heritage Coast'.

Durlston Castle,
c. 1930.

SWANAGE

The Lock-up

Immediately behind the town hall is the town's original lock-up – a (very) small, windowless stone building with a heavy, iron-studded door and, inside, a fixed wooden bench for the benefit of those individuals having to 'cool off' for the night. Over the door is this rather sanctimoniously worded inscription: 'For the Prevention of Vice and Immorality by the Friends of Religion and Good Order'. But then, it was originally erected in 1803 in the churchyard, and was moved to this position probably because it would have been handier for the Town Constable. Any 'inhabitant' could have his 'morning after' thirst slaked from either a nearby stone water conduit or from a massive cast-iron pump – he would most likely have needed plenty of water to swill out his night's lodging in the lock-up!

The lock-up with a massive cast-iron hand pump on the right; a stone conduit on the left and a London lamppost.

78

Map Ref
ST 375033

THORNCOMBE

The SS Collars

Inside the church of St Mary the Virgin in Thorncombe, now safely under glass to protect it from brass rubbing, is reputedly the finest monumental brass in England. It depicts Sir Thomas (b. 1419) and Lady Brook lying side by side with a small dog at Sir Thomas' feet. Sir Thomas wears the usual belted gown of the period and has a buckled 'Lancastrian Collar', bearing the letters 'SS', around his neck. Lady Brook wears a kirtle and mantle, a distinctive horned head-dress and a similar collar. Even the little dog wears the same collar but without the 'SS'! The four shields on the brass are unadorned. The depiction of these collars is extremely rare, and there have, in the past, been disputes as to the meaning of 'SS'. The interpretations of 'SS' as being *Spiritus Sanctus* or *Senschellus* (Steward) of England have both since been discounted. They are now believed to show that the wearer was loyal to the Lancastrian cause and represent an Order founded by John of Gaunt (1340–99). He gave the collar to his nephew, Richard II (1377–97), after which it was adopted by Henry IV (1399–1413), who granted it to many adherents of the Lancastrian cause, especially those attached to the court.

The brass was removed from the old church of St Mary when the new church was built in 1887, with a replica brass beside the old one from which rubbings can be taken.

Sir Thomas, who came from Brooke, near Ilchester in Somerset, married Joan, 2nd Baroness of Cobham in Kent, and settled in the manor-house at Holditch, about 3 miles from Thorncombe (see **33**).

The brass of
Sir Thomas and
Lady Brook in the
church of St Mary
the Virgin at
Thorncombe.
*(Thorncombe
Parochial Church
Council)*

79

Map Ref
SZ 589186

TRENT

The Hiding Place

After his defeat at Worcester on 3 September 1651 Charles Stuart, the future King Charles II, was a wanted man with a price of £1,000 on his head, and in need of a safe refuge until he could join his mother, Queen Henrietta, in France. Col Francis Wyndham of Trent Manor, near Sherborne, offered this, and Charles, in the disguise of a servant riding before Mrs Jane Lane, accompanied by Cornet Henry Lasselles, arrived there on the 17th. (As most journeys were then on horseback, ladies usually rode pillion behind a servant, who 'rode before'.) At Trent there was a 6ft square room above the brewhouse in which Charles could hide should the occasion arise. Its little window was hidden by other buildings and the door was concealed behind a staircase and could only be entered through a tiny space beneath the stairs. Should this room be likely to be discovered then there was a second, though far less comfortable hiding place: a 4ft deep void beneath the floorboards, entered by lifting two of the boards.

The stairs have since been removed, thus fully exposing the doorway, and because surrounding buildings have been demolished the little window is now visible.

Trent is never open to the public.

The little window, now exposed, of Charles Stuart's hiding place at Trent Manor.

The door into
the hiding
place. *(Mrs
G. Hohler)*

80

Map Ref
ST 594185

TRENT

Vanity, Vanity . . .

It is here in St Andrew's Church that Sir Francis and Lady Ann Wyndham lie buried, recorded by a simple tablet low on the south wall of the north chapel. All the families who lived at Trent Manor would have used the railed-off section of the north aisle, and the ladies, just as today, would have tried to look their best when they attended services. On the underside of the arch dividing the north aisle from the nave is an inscription from Isaiah 6: 40 and Psalm 15: 103. It is, however, in mirror writing, so that those vain enough to use their 'looking glasses' in church would have been reminded of their religious duties and been mildly chided for their vanity!

In the porch of
St Andrew's
Church at Trent.

ALL FLESH IS GRASSE AND THE GLORY
OF IS AS THE FLOURE OF THE FIELDE

Would these same ladies, however, have worn the pattens and clogs the other worshippers had to take off before entering the church by the west door, as instructed by the notice there?

The church's golden weathercock of 1698 is pierced by several small, round holes, made by musket balls fired by high-spirited sportsmen keen to show off their marksmanship. Unlike the cock on St Mary's Church, at Ottery St Mary in Devon, which was used for target practice by Col Fairfax's troops in 1644.

A drawing of a weathercock by Alan Patchett. *(Trent Parochial Council)*

TYNEHAM

The Lost Village

In 1943 the army tank training camps at Bovington and East Lulworth needed to extend their firing range near the coast east of Lulworth but were prevented by the presence of a village – Tyneham. So, with the promise of being able to return once the war was over, the entire village was evacuated, lock, stock and barrel. They were never allowed to return, however, and today the little village consists only of the ruins of the houses and farmsteads, overgrown fields and orchards and neglected sheep runs. The church had survived and it now serves as an information centre with the graveyard being kept neat. Unusually for an area rich in stone, many of the late nineteenth-century graves have cast-iron grave markers, 'off the peg' from a Somerset foundry. There is, however, a surprising survivor in the village, an extremely rare example of a No. 1 Design GPO telephone call box!

The telephone box at Tyneham. *(Peter Stanier)*

When firing on the ranges is not taking place the surrounding roads and footpaths are opened to the public so that the village can be visited, and, owing to the lack of cultivation, the ¾-mile walk down to Warborrow Bay can be enjoyed for its abundant wildlife. There is a car park at Tyneham – fee optional.

Dorset has another unusual telephone call box: at Okeford Fitzpaine, where the inhabitants insist that instead of the traditional red it is painted green!

82

Map Ref
SY 660851

UPWEY

The 'Wishing Well'

It is not strictly a well at all but the welling up into a 5ft deep limestone bowl of two strong springs where the permeable Portland stone and sand meets the impermeable Kimmeridge clay; the summertime flow of 1½ million gallons of water per day being the headwaters of the 5-mile long River Wey.

Used by the village as its water supply, when Weymouth became a fashionable 'watering place' in the eighteenth century, the 'well' was a quaintly rustic place to visit. It did not, however, become the more romantic-sounding 'wishing well' until the 1870s, when it became widely known, with visitors coming by train (Upwey Halt), wagonette and, later, charabanc. A custom grew up for a glassful to be taken, sipped, a wish made, and the remainder to be thrown back into the stream. The arcaded stone shelter and seat were erected by George Thomas Ingleheim Gould, the owner of the estate, to commemorate the Golden Jubilee of Queen Victoria in 1887. His initials are over the arcade.

King George III is reputed to have drunk the water here on one of his many visits to Weymouth and it was reported in the local newspapers that Queen Charlotte visited the well in 1798 and 1801; HRH Edward, Prince of Wales sipped the water in 1923, although his wish was not recorded – fourteen years later it could have been guessed at!

Visiting the well and drinking its water is still free, the grounds below the well is now a charming water-garden and refreshments can be taken at the tea-rooms. Some twenty years ago the delightful, yearly Derbyshire custom of well dressing was introduced, and long may it continue.

The 'wishing well', c. 1906.

WEST BAY

The 'Resort' that never was

For centuries the harbour serving Bridport – Bridport Quay – was the estuary of the little River Brit, but this could never have been easy for ships either to enter or to leave as the river's mouth was between shifting banks of shingle. Because of this Bridport Quay never had the importance or the trade as did Lyme Regis, which was once the sixth largest port in England. Between 1740 and 1774 two jetties were built out into the sea to protect the river mouth and to make the entrance more navigable. The harbour itself was enlarged in 1824 but it never became a viable proposition for larger ocean-going vessels and, when trade and ship-building declined dramatically during the latter half of the nineteenth century, so did the fortune of the harbour.

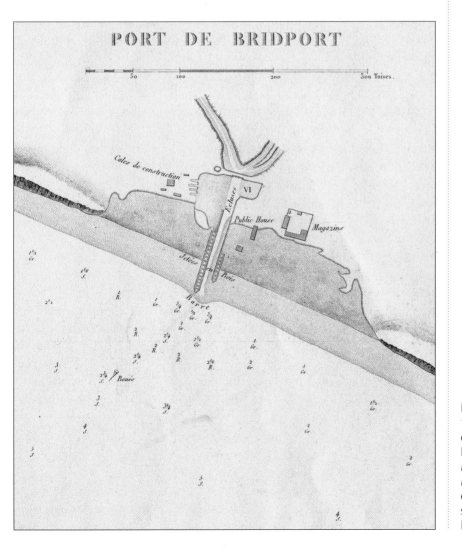

Bridport on an 1824 French copy of one of Lieutenant Murdock Mackensie's charts of the south coast of England.

Men hauling a
vessel out of
trouble off
Bridport Harbour;
by J.M.W. Turner,
from his
*Picturesque Views
of the South
Coast of England*
(1814).

In 1857 the Great Western Railway opened its line between Castle
Cary and Weymouth, with the Bridport Railway Company (taken over
by the GWR in 1901) building a branch line from Maiden Newton to
Bridport which, in 1884, was extended to Bridport Quay. Not, however,
to carry goods but because the railway company thought the locality
was ripe for development into a 'resort' as had happened to
Bournemouth earlier in the century. The company insisted that
Bridport Quay be renamed more invitingly West Bay, with the first
development, an imposing terrace of four large houses and an hotel
being built to the east of the harbour in 1884. A Grand Esplanade was
planned for the west of the harbour and this was opened in 1887.

In spite of the glorious surrounding scenery, the bracing air and the
good and safe swimming, the expected 'boom' did not materialise –
they were too late and West Bay did not attract either sufficient
visitors or fashionable residents. A report in 1915 said: 'the district
does not draw many long-distance travellers' then more hopefully
'but when a small sea-side resort becomes of sufficient importance . . .
it will not be long before the place earns an extended reputation'. From
the railway company's point of view it never did; the line to West Bay
closed to passengers during the First World War and completely in
1930. Sporadic development took place over the years along the
Esplanade, but although West Bay now attracts the retired, caravans,
campers and day visitors, the harbour remains the prime attraction
and it cannot be said in any way to have become the 'resort'

envisaged. In this respect it is similar to the much larger and grandly optimistic Silloth, on the Solway Firth in Cumbria; except that while the sea is always attractive at West Bay, at Silloth it can only be seen twice a day – at high tide!

West Bay from the east, c. 1905, showing very little development.

West Bay from the west, c. 1930; still little development.

84

Map Ref
S 67/68

WEYMOUTH

Sea Bathing

In 1763 Ralph Allen, a prosperous stage coach owner and mail deliverer of Bath, was recommended by his doctor to undergo a revolutionary treatment for his (unspecified) complaint: 'to immerse his bare body in the sea'! He went to Weymouth, then a small port, took the treatment and was cured; this 'cure' became fashionable and Weymouth was changed for ever. Allen probably turned his knowledge of coach-building to devising a 'bathing machine', which could be trundled into the sea and allow the occupant to bathe in comfort and modesty.

The reputation of Weymouth as a 'watering place' was confirmed when, between 1789 and 1805, King George III, Queen Charlotte and their whole family came every year for the 'cure', staying at the Duke of Gloucester's house on the Esplanade. When the King first immersed himself from his massive 'bathing machine' a band had been positioned and struck up 'God Save the King' – he must have needed the encouragement, for by then the 'cure' included drinking a quantity of sea water every day. He had a marble bath installed in the house so that during inclement weather he could continue his sea water treatment. Both the 'bathing machine' and the marble bath can still be seen in Weymouth's 'Timewalk'.

The crowds still come to Weymouth to enjoy the sea and sands, but they no longer drink the water and are far less modest.

Weymouth beach, c. 1905, with the bathing machines still in use.

WHITCHURCH CANONICORUM

85

Map Ref
ST 396954

The Shrine of St Wite

There are many stories about who St Wite (pronounced Wita) was, her sainthood and how she came to be buried in and give her name to the church of St Candida (St Wite) and Holy Cross at Whitchurch Canonicorum. Suffice it to say that her tomb has been a shrine of pilgrimage for hundreds of years – the only other shrine in the country which has survived intact being that of Edward the Confessor at Westminster Abbey. St Wite became widely known for her power in healing the sick, with pilgrims coming from far and near to offer up prayers at her tomb, placing personal articles, offerings of money or even an afflicted part of their body in one of the three oval openings in the stone support beneath the tomb. Others would bring a piece of clothing or a small personal possession from someone who was too sick to travel. Often the pilgrims would go to Chardown Hill, above Morcombelake, to drink the water from the Holy Well of St Wite, or to bathe their eyes if they were suffering from an eye affliction. This belief in the efficacy of the well's water to cure eye complaints continued into the twentieth century and the well is today tended carefully. In 1900, when repairs had to be carried out to the church

The tomb of
St Wite.

✠hⲓC·REꝊ·ESCT·RELIꝊE · SCE · WITE·

" Here rest the remains of S. Wite."

fabric and to the tomb itself, a small, 2ft 5in × 8in square, lead reliquary box was uncovered in the tomb. It was found to contain the bones of a small woman and in raised lettering on the one undamaged side of the reliquary was inscribed with the above words.

The tracks that can be seen in the sea off the cliffs of Golden Cap – caused by the changing temperature of the strong currents there – were, within living memory, known as 'St Wite's Tracks' and were once thought to mark the course of her passage across the Channel from France.

WIMBORNE MINSTER

The Astronomical Clock

86

Map Ref
SZ 008999

On the south wall of the baptistry in the west tower of the Minster Church of St Cuthberga is an astronomical clock that has been ticking away the years since the fourteenth century (or rather, the works in the tower have, for the movement is transferred down to the 'dial' via rods). It was first mentioned in the Churchwarden's Account of 1409, when a case was made for the 'dial' with 'a little lock and key', and again in 1425 when repairs were made to 'le clok'. It was made before Copernicus proposed the theory that the earth circled the sun, when 'dials' had no hands but showed the sun circling the earth during a 24-hour period. The 'dial' at St Cuthberga's is described by Edward Stanham MA as:

The earth, represented by a green ball at the centre, around which the moon revolves against a black night sky dotted with silver stars; the moon also revolves on its own axis, changing colour from silver to black to mark its phases. Against the outer ring of the blue sky, revolves the golden symbol for the sun, marking the hours against 22 Roman numerals in black on gold round the edge of the dial. A cross at the top indicates midday and another at the bottom marking mid-night. There is nothing to show the minutes which have to be estimated by the position of the sun symbol between the hours.

The astronomical clock at Wimborne Minster.

The sundial.

'The Jack', dressed as a grenadier guardsman.

The present case and ornamentations are eighteenth-century. There are three similar astronomical clocks in the West Country – in Exeter Cathedral, Wells Cathedral and St Mary's at Ottery St Mary in Devon.

The 'clock' in the ringing chamber also activates a marionette – here called 'The Jack' – who sits on the outside north face of the west tower. 'The Jack' hits two bells to sound the quarter hours with one, two or three strikes, and with four strikes on the hours. He is now dressed as a grenadier guardsman of 1815.

Clocks of that period did not keep very accurate time and would have needed constant adjustment, but how? Outside the west tower on its south side is a 9ft-high square stone column, on the top of which is a 4ft × 3ft × 6ft-high sundial, with gnomons on three of its sides. This was formerly on the gable of the south transept and bears the date 1752, but there would have been another before that.

87

Map Ref
SU 032119

WIMBORNE ST GILES

Memorials to Love and Devotion

When the roof of St Giles' Church was removed for repairs in 1887, a pair of robins built their nest near the altar. As robins were considered holy (they were supposed to have lain on Christ's breast while he was hanging on the Cross to comfort him, with the blood from his wounds staining their little breasts red for evermore), the workmen did not disturb the pair until the fledglings had flown. They then put the nest in a glass jar and sealed it up in a hole in the church wall. Twenty years later an odd thing happened; a fire had damaged a part of the roof and once again a pair of robins nested near the altar. When the brood had hatched and flown, this nest in turn was put into the same remembered hole in the church wall. It was then that the decorated memorial panel was put up on the east wall near the altar to commemorate the events.

For generations Wimborne St Giles had been the country home of the Earls of Shaftesbury, and when the 7th Earl died a memorial was erected in 1893 to his memory. It is the fountain in the centre of Piccadilly Circus, probably the best-known memorial in the whole country, surmounted by a statue of Eros, the Greek god of love, although in this case symbolising Christian charity. A long way from Wimborne St Giles' but Eros was set up so that his arrow is aimed directly towards that small village in Dorset.

The decorated memorial panel to the nesting robins, near the altar in St Giles' Church, Wimborne St Giles.

WINFRITH NEWBURGH

Scratch or Mass Dials

88

Map Ref
SY 804843

Cut into the stone arch and jambs of the small priest's door, on the south side of St Christopher's Church, are three very worn sets of radiating lines, with a shallow indentation at the centre of each. Possibly Norman in origin, these scratch or 'Mass' dials are now rare survivors, used, and probably cut, by the priest long before the age of clocks. They enabled him to know when to conduct the services, especially Mass, and for the bell-ringer to know when to summon the worshippers. From fragments found in other parts of the country (none have survived whole) the central indentations (holes) would have held short upright iron rods or 'styles' which acted as primitive gnomons, casting their shadows on the incised lines. As an upright 'style' would have only told the correct time for a short period of the year, other dials were incised with bent or angled 'styles', so telling the time at other seasons of the year, which accounts for the number of dials at St Christopher's.

Two of the three scratch dials on St Christopher's Church, Winfrith Newburgh.

The priest would have made these dials by trial and error, first scratching a horizontal line at the equinox with the 'style' at its centre, one end of the line representing 6 a.m., the other 6 p.m. When the sun was thought to be at its zenith at midday, a scratch would be made where the 'style' cast its shadow, thus creating two segments, each segment was then divided by five equi-distant scratches to give the hours from 6 a.m. to 6 p.m. Probably many experimental marks would be scratched before the priest was satisfied that he had made the dial correctly, when he would then incise the final scratches more deeply – the lines seen today.

Scratch dials have also been found on the church of St Candia at Whitchurch Canonicorum and St Peter and St Paul at Mappowder.

89

Map Ref
ST 774069

WOOLLAND

The Studio of Dame Elisabeth Frink

Deep in the Dorset countryside below Bulbarrow Hill lies hidden the converted stable block of the former Woolland House, which was for many years the home of Dame Elisabeth Frink, one of the foremost twentieth-century sculptors. Here she lived from 1976 with her third husband, Alex Csaky, and had her studio in the beautiful and extensive grounds. These still contain many of her works: groups and single figures of the male nude (a favourite subject at one time), symbolic heads and shapes and life-like animals. There is also a delightful life-size sculpture of Dame Elisabeth by F.E. MacWilliam.

Cornwall makes much of Dame Barbara Hepworth at St Ives and it is a great shame that Dame Elisabeth is not as widely known in Dorset. Her only work that can be seen in the county by the public is her group, 'The Dorset Martyrs', on the site of the old gallows in South Walk, Dorchester, commissioned in 1986. However, the work that she considered her most satisfying, 'The Walking Madonna', can be seen on Salisbury Cathedral Green. Unusually the Madonna is not holding the Christ child but is depicted walking away from the Cross, with her face showing the grief of any mother who has just lost her child.

Dame Elisabeth Frink's studio at Woolland.

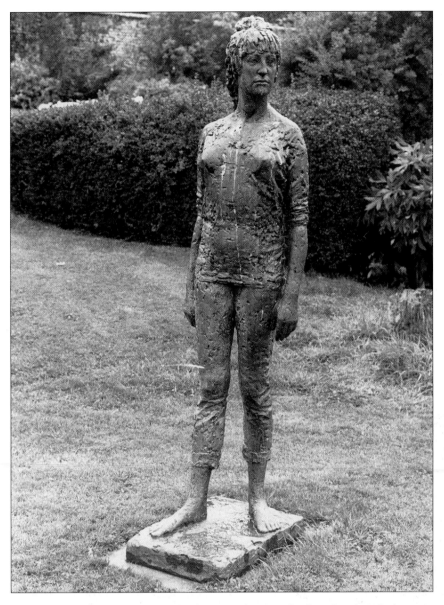

Sculpture of
Dame Elisabeth
by F.E. MacWilliam
in the grounds.

The studio is almost as she last used it, with the clay head she was working on now cracking and crumbling, a maquette of the Dorset Martyrs and the walls with scribbled notes of telephone numbers and the names of pieces of music she had been listening to on the wireless. She worked tirelessly until the end, even going to the casting foundry to supervise the completion of her last commission, 'Risen Christ', for Liverpool Cathedral.

She died in 1993 and until the funeral her coffin rested on the largest work-table in her studio.

The studio and grounds are not open to the general public but can be visited by arrangement, through Blandford Forum Tourist Information Centre.

90

WORTH MATRAVERS

The Grave of Benjamin Jesty

In the churchyard of St Nicholas is the gravestone of farmer Benjamin Jesty (1737–1816) and that of his wife, Elizabeth (1740–1824). Unlikely as it seems Benjamin must be included in the annals for the advancement in medical knowledge during the eighteenth century; the simple inscription on his headstone reads: 'an upright and honest man, particularly noted for being the first person (known) that introduced the Cow Pox by inoculation, and who from his great strength of mind, made the experiment from the cow on his wife and two sons in 1774'.

Dr Jenner, of Berkeley in Gloucestershire, is generally credited with the first inoculation, and it was indeed he who continued and perfected this practice of protection against smallpox. However, for a long time farmers had observed that cowmen and milkmaids who contracted the relatively mild cowpox (which brought out a few weeping spots or pocks) seemed not to succumb to the disfiguring and often fatal smallpox, which killed between 10 and 20 per cent of the population at that time and accounted for one in three deaths of children.

Benjamin Jesty's headstone at St Nicholas' Church, Worth Matravers.

Benjamin, who at that time was farming at Yetminster in Dorset, 'using a steel knitting needle and the pus from a pustule on a cow's udder' 'enoculated' (*sic*) his family against smallpox by giving them cowpox (presumably they also had great strength of mind!). In the church at Worth Matravers is a tablet to a lady which mentions that Benjamin had 'enoculated' her and it is highly likely that he performed this service on many others.

In 1796, when Dr Jenner had proved the theory by giving a milkmaid a deliberate infection of smallpox after she had developed cowpox and from which she suffered no ill effects, Jenner attempted to decry Benjamin's experiments. However, the medical profession had in the end to credit Benjamin with being the first, inviting him to London to speak before the 'Vaccine Pock Institution', when they also commissioned a portrait of him.

WORTH MATRAVERS

St Aldhelm's Chapel

91

Map Ref
SY 960755

Just over a mile from the village this stone-built Norman chapel, dating from about 1200, is only 32ft square and stands atop the towering 350ft high cliffs of St Aldhelm's Head. It is said to have been built by a father who, watching his daughter and her husband sailing down the Channel to a new home, saw the boat wrecked in a sudden storm with all on board being drowned. As it is not built east/west but has its four corners facing the four main points of the compass, it was in all likelihood not built as a chapel but as a home for a hermit. There is a small platform on the apex of the roof which once would have held a cresset, or brazier, lit and tended by the hermit to warn shipping of this dangerous shore (there are other instances of such 'lighthouses' around our coasts). When the building was converted into a chapel dedicated to St Aldhelm (who built Sherborne Abbey), the altar had to be positioned awkwardly across the north-east corner and the cresset replaced by a cross.

The only light inside is provided by a small slit-window facing seaward (where the hermit would have watched for shipping) and the stone roof is supported by a central pillar; there is a hole in this in which alms could have been placed. However, the chapel later became known as a 'wishing chapel', the wish being granted when something personal, such as a pin, was placed in the hole.

During the nineteenth century regular Sunday services were held there for the coastguards who lived in the nearby cottages and an Easter service continued for many years.

St Aldhelm's Chapel.

WYKE

St George's Church

92

Map Ref
ST 788265

Memorials to the dead of the First World War tend to be unimaginative, if worthy, monolithic blocks of stone. This one at Langham is one of the exceptions; here the memorial to the fallen of the hamlet and the neighbouring estate is a little thatched church, St George's, built in 1921 and set among trees on the road to Gillingham. It was designed by Ponting in simple Arts and Crafts style and sits snugly under its thatch and little steeple, and is one of only a handful of such thatched churches in the country.

It is now only used at festivals and for special occasions and is normally kept locked.

St George's Church.

<table>
<tr><td>

93

Map Ref
SY 672777

</td></tr>
</table>

WYKE REGIS

The Smuggler

During the eighteenth and first half of the nineteenth centuries the Dorset coast was wide open to smugglers working off the French coast from Roscoff to Dieppe. The men bringing in the silks, brandy, tea and tobacco were, in reality, rough and violent, who were ready to fight the 'preventative men' should the occasion arise, or any others for that matter, to protect their territory, much as modern drug traffickers do today.

Because of poverty, fear or just because they were 'agin authority' many local people connived at the smuggling or turned a blind eye to it, for as the saying went, 'look to the wall, my darling, when the "gentlemen" go by'. Once that kind of lawlessness ceased, smuggling became romanticised, albeit based on some half-forgotten fact: public houses were renamed the Smugglers Inn (at Osmington); any isolated cottage near the coast became Smuggler's Cottage (at Ringstead); remote tracks coming up from the beach were called Smugglers Lane or Path (on Stonebarrow Hill) and tales grew around any cave or likely hiding place for contraband (the quarries at Tilly Whim).

But there are very few tangible remains – except one stark reminder of the risks which smugglers took. In the churchyard at Wyke Regis there is a headstone erected to an 'Affectionate Husband' by his wife, with the representation of the confrontation between a smuggler's boat and the Revenue Schooner *Pigmy*, with these words: 'Sacred to the Memory of William Lewis who was killed by a shot from the "Pigmy" Schooner 21st April 1822. Aged 33 years.' In further lines William is made to say 'Repent all, ere it be too late' and pleads

This sketch map shows the stretches of English coastline supplied by smugglers from French ports. From Smuggling Days and Smuggling Ways.

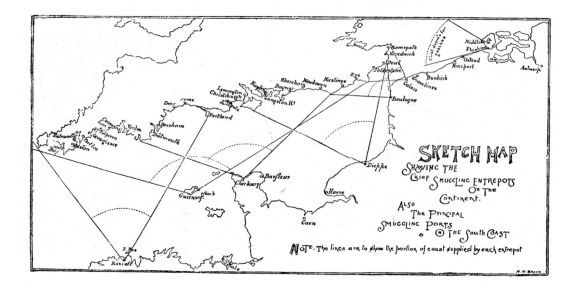

Smuggler's Cottage in Ringstead Bay, *c.* 1910.

Tillywhim Caves, *c.* 1930.

'To save me on the Judgement Day'. However, just over the border in Devon, at Branscombe, it was a 'preventative man', John Hurley, who met a violent death, which is also recorded on his headstone.

Drawing of the carving on William Lewis' headstone depicting the occasion of his death, from *Smuggling Days and Smuggling Ways.*

BIBLIOGRAPHY AND FURTHER READING

Barker, K., *Sherborne*, Abbey Press, 1982

Bickley, C., *Where Dorset Meets Devon*, London, Constable, 1911

Charmouth Pavey Group, *Journals. The Village Echo*, 1999–

Cochrane, C., *The Lost Roads of Wessex*, Pan, 1969

Cooksey, A.J.A., *Admiralty Signal and Telegraph Stations*, 1974

Cooper, A.T.P., *Benjamin Jesty 1737–1816*, Dorset Natural History and Archaeological Society, 1969

Cox, B., *Book of Blandford*, Barracuda, 1983

Davies, G.M., *The Dorset Coast. A Geological Guide*, 2nd edn, A. & C. Black, 1956

Draper, J., *Dorset. The Complete Guide*, Dovecote Press, 1992

Draper, J., *Proceedings Dorset Natural History & Archaeological Society Vol. 123*, 2001

Eedle, M. de G., *History of Beaminster*, Phillimore, 1984

Farrugia, J., *The Letter Box*, Centaur Press, 1969

French, G., *Stoke Abbott*, Creeds, Bridport, 1974

Fuller, Revd Thomas, *The Worthies of England*, London, 1662

Gardiner, S., *Official Biography of Elisabeth Frink*, HarperCollins, 1998

Good, R., *The Old Roads of Dorset*, Longman, 1940

Hamilton, R., *Now I Remember*, Pan, 1968

Hawkes, C. & J., *Prehistoric Britain*, Penguin, 1943

Headley, G. & Meulenkamp, W., *Follies*, Jonathan Cape, 1986

Hine, R., *Beaminster*, Wessex Press, 1914

Hutchins, J., *History of Dorset*, J.B. Nichols & Son, 1867

Innes, B., *Shaftesbury. A Pictorial History*, Dovecote Press, 1992

Kelly, A., *Mrs Coade's Stone*, Self Publishing Association, 1990

Legg, R., *The Jurassic Coast*, Dorset Publishing Co., 2002

Mee, A., *The King's England. Dorset*, Hodder & Stoughton, 1967

Newman, J. & Pevsner, N., *The Buildings of England. Dorset*, Penguin, 1986

Osborn, G.H., *Proceedings Dorset Natural History & Archaeological Society Vol. 104*, 1982

Osborne, C., *Dorset Curiosities*, Wimborne, 1986

Phillips, M., *Picture of Lyme Regis*, Dunster, Lyme Regis, 1817

Roberts, C., *History of Lyme Regis*, Samuel Bagster, 1834

Shore, H.N. Com. The Hon. RN, *Smuggling Days and Smuggling Ways*, Cassell, London, 1892

Stanham, E., MA, *The Astronomical Clock at Wimborne Minster*, E. Stanham, 1988

Stanier, Dr P., *Dorset in the Age of Steam*, Dorset Books, Hallsgrove, 2002

Thomas, D. St J., *Regional History of the Railways. The West Country*, David & Charles, 1960

Timpson, J., *Timpson's England*, Jarrold, 1991

Treves, Sir F., *Highways and Byways in Dorset*, MacMillan, 1906

Waters, Christine, *Who was St. Wite?*, Creeds, 1980

Church Notes: Bridport (Friends), Chideock (RC), East Lulworth (RC), Mappowder, Melbury Bubb, Moreton, Portisham, Puncknowle, Thorncombe, Trent, Whitchurch Canonicorum

ACKNOWLEDGEMENTS

I should like to thank all those who have helped me during my research and on my visits: Viv Harrison, Upwey; Mrs D. Hawkins, Frampton; Judy Lindsay, Dorset County Museum; Margaret Livingston, Colyton; Mrs P. Tolley, Holditch; Anthony Allcock, Weymouth Museum; Revd A. Ashwell, Litton Cheney; staff of Bridport County Library; David Bromwich, Librarian, Somerset Archaeological and Natural History Society; Dr S.D. Chapman, Manchester; Revd E. Chivers, Thorncombe; staff of Dorset Reference Library; Roger Eckersley, Wellington; Charles Eyres, Sadborow; Revd R. Fairbrother, Whitchurch Canonicorum; Dr Michael Glanvill, Chard; Mike Jones, Taunton; Officer in Waiting, College of Heralds, London; Revd G. Perryman and Moreton Parochial Church Council; Mr M. Potter, Frampton; Peter Press, Charmouth; John Radford, Wimborne St Giles; the Manager, Riviera Hotel, Bowleaze; Alex Selbie, Shaftesbury Historical Society; Dr Peter Stanier, Shaftesbury; Charles Weld, Chideock; Wilfrid Weld, Lulworth Castle, and Adrian Wood, Palmer's Brewery, Bridport. My special thanks must go to Liz-Ann Bawden, Lyme Regis, who showed me the old wooden letter-box; Mrs G. Hohler, Trent Manor, for allowing me access to Charles Stuart's hiding place; Brenda Innes, Shaftesbury, who told me of the 'Byzant'; Louise Perrin, Russell-Cotes Museum and Art Gallery, for her guidance and suggestions; Lim Jammet, Woolland, for giving me such free access to the studio of his late mother, Dame Elisabeth Frink, and to Mr E.J. Ward, Morcombelake, who pointed me to the jaw-bone arch at Chideock.